TERESE ALLEN

BOUNTIFUL
WISCONSIN

110 FAVORITE RECIPES

Trails Books
Black Earth, Wisconsin

Library of Congress Catalog Card Number: 99-69921
ISBN: 0-915024-78-0

Editor: Stan Stoga
Design and production: Impressions Book and Journal Services, Inc.
Cover design: Kate Orenberg
Cover photo: Paskus Photography
Back cover photo: Jack Kloppenburg

Printed in the United States of America.
06 05 04 03 02 01 00   6 5 4 3 2 1

TRAILS BOOKS, a division of
Trails Media Group, Inc.
P.O. Box 317
Black Earth, WI 53515

(800) 236-8088   e-mail: info@wistrails.com
www.trailsbooks.com

To "The Quilters," who really cook,
eat, drink, talk, laugh, and listen.

In memory of Laure

ACKNOWLEDGMENTS

Thank you to all the marvelous cooks of Wisconsin and beyond who contributed to this book. A big gracias also to Lucia Allen-Voreis and Claire Reinke, who helped with recipe testing (yet again); to the folks at Trails Media Group for taking on this project; and, most of all, to JB (that tall, good-looking, bearded guy).

CONTENTS

INTRODUCTION

In the late 1990s, the editors of *Wisconsin Trails* magazine sponsored two recipe contests that highlighted our state's crops and products. Cooks from Wisconsin and around the United States entered more than five hundred recipes, thirty of which won prizes and a spot in my column, "Wisconsin Cuisine" (now called "Dining In").

The 1997 competition featured picnic foods, popular with many locals who love a good tailgate party and know how to make the most of the state's all-too-brief summers. The five entry categories were appetizers, salads, side dishes, main dishes, and desserts. In 1998 the contest theme hit even closer to the heart of Wisconsin by emphasizing its agricultural heritage; the recipe categories were apples, cherries, berries, dairy products, potatoes, beef, and pork. Each year the judges, a very lucky panel of tasters from the Wisconsin Trails staff, rated the recipes on such criteria as originality, best use of Badger State products, presentation and visual appeal, clarity of directions, ease of preparation, and of course, taste. Given the large number of entries, the judges had a tough job but insisted they were very glad to do it. In all, thirteen recipes were declared winners and seventeen received honorable mentions.

But it seemed a shame to let so many other worthy recipes go unrecognized, and thus was born the idea for this book. The folks at Trails told me that my mission—should I decide to accept it—was to sort through the recipes, gather the best one hundred or so (including the contest winners), then test and edit them for publication. Accept the mission? I felt like the proverbial kid in the candy store—with a gift certificate in hand.

At first, my goal was simple: hatch a collection of delicious, original, and easy-to-follow recipes from the teetering pile. But then, as the chapters formed and the book took shape, I began to notice themes within the recipes—patterns of ethnic traditions, agricultural influences, international flavors, streamlined cooking methods, health and environmental awareness, and more. I realized that what I was actually working on was a treasury of home cooking in Wisconsin today.

One theme really stood out among the others: the very friendliness of Wisconsin food. Here, contemporary home cooking is about wholesome dishes that are prepared and presented informally but graciously. Here, "homemade" means the kind of local, seasonal cooking that is less about trendsetting and more about simple country goodness.

In *Calling the Midwest Home* Carolyn Lieberg wrote, "Somebody with an interesting computer program figured out that one-third of Americans live within five hundred miles of Wisconsin. All I can say is, if they all decide to visit, everybody in the state better put the coffeepot on."

The thing is, here in Wisconsin, we already have.

Terese Allen

1

APPETIZERS and SOUPS

Ask most newcomers to Wisconsin what impresses them most about the state, and "the friendliness of the people" is usually at the top of their list. Around here, when someone says "How-ya-doin'?" it's an actual question. In a car, four fingers lifted briefly from the arc of the steering wheel isn't a traffic signal or a motorist shooing a fly, it's the on-the-road version of "Howdy," and if you're a visitor to someone's home, you're likely to be greeted with a hug and a plateful of summer sausage and cheese.

Starting Signals

In Wisconsin, as elsewhere, appetizers are a way of saying "Welcome." They reassure guests that they're wanted. Appetizers establish trust. Hosts know that a chunky fresh salsa or a savory broccoli cheddar dip is to an arriving diner as bait is to a jumpy fish. Dishes like these and others in this section lure a visitor in and distract her from the fear of being a bad guest. They give her something to do: dip a cracker, pass a napkin, sip some wine. She's beguiled by the colorful layers in a pesto torta or the smoky scent of a whitefish spread, and in just a nibble or two, she's hooked. She's relaxed and having a good time.

Like the flattering tidbits of information about ourselves that we offer to a new friend, appetizers show our best side first. No wonder, then, that in the Dairy State hors d'oeuvres so often mean cheese. With some 250 Wisconsin varieties (and counting) the prospects are many: from standards like colby and cheddar to organic and low-fat choices for the health conscious; and from old-time favorites like limburger to upscale specialties such as gorgonzola and smoked gouda. If appetizers bespeak the pleasures that lie ahead, then a first course prepared with top-quality Wisconsin cheese predicts a feast indeed.

Comfort Zone

Soup supplies its own kind of welcome. Like a steamy bath or a late night mug of hot chocolate, a bowl of beefy mushroom barley or sausage corn chowder, both featured in this chapter, offers warmth and liquid solace.

Soup comforts us just when we need it most. When plummeting temperatures threaten and we're faced with our white, wintery limits, a stockpot is an opportunity, a reminder that anything is possible. For a soup cook, there are no checks on the fresh, frozen, and processed ingredients, the ethnic and cultural influences, and the soup varieties she can access. In the recipes that follow, the cook transforms rigid potatoes and cauliflower into a creamy purée of roast vegetables and stirs chewy, earthy-tasting wild rice into a broth studded with pork and vegetables, revealing that when a soup maker makes soup, she reintroduces color, texture, aroma, and compassion to life.

Bisque, chowder, chili, panade, and consommé all sustain us and strengthen our resolve. Part of upper midwestern lore is the ability to withstand extreme weather, to survive against all odds. Wisconsinites are famous not just for their ability to endure the interminable winter but for their capacity to enjoy it, even to laugh in its face. We're tough, and proud of it.

The secret is preparation. Just as we hang storm windows, tighten ski bindings, and knit bulky scarves, so do we slice onions and simmer broth. And just as we bask in the warmth of a crackling fire built from logs we cut ourselves, so do we savor a long-simmered batch of soup, patiently prepared and eaten the second day, when maximum flavor has developed.

PESTO TORTA

Cream the cream cheese, butter, parmesan, and garlic in a bowl. Place 1 cup of this mixture into a smaller bowl; fold the pesto into this until well blended. Line a 1-quart bowl or mold with overlapping layers of plastic wrap, flattening the plastic against the sides of the dish. Pack the "plain" cream cheese mixture into the bottom of the lined dish, spreading it to level the top. Spread the cream cheese–pesto mixture over this, again making it level. Fold the plastic wrap over the torta and chill until firm, 4 to 6 hours.

To make topping: Place dried tomatoes in a bowl and pour ⅔ cup boiling water over them. Weight the tomatoes with a small plate to submerge them, then let them steep until soft, about 20 minutes. Drain well (the liquid can be used to flavor soups or sauces); chop the tomatoes and set aside. Roast the red peppers on a long fork over an open flame, turning often, until the entire skin is black and blistered. Allow peppers to cool briefly, then scrape off all the blackened skin with a sharp knife. Cut peppers in half, remove all the seeds, then coarsely chop the "meat." (Alternatively, you may substitute chopped black olives for the roasted red pepper.) Combine the tomatoes and red peppers or black olives; stir in olive oil and black pepper to taste.

When torta is fully chilled, unfold the plastic wrap, turn torta out onto a serving platter, and remove the plastic wrap. Spoon topping over torta. Serve with crackers or sliced baguette.

Makes 12 to 16 servings.

2 packages (each 8 ounces) cream cheese, softened

½ cup (1 stick) butter, softened

½ cup freshly grated parmesan cheese

2 to 3 teaspoons minced garlic, mashed to a paste with fork or flat of knife

3 tablespoons basil (or cilantro) pesto

½ cup dried tomatoes

⅔ cup boiling water

2 medium red bell peppers or 1 cup imported black olives, pitted and chopped

2 tablespoons olive oil

freshly ground black pepper

VICKI DUEMLER, BRODHEAD, WISCONSIN

"This is a wonder spread for a party, the beginning of an Italian dinner, or any festive occasion, even as part of a soup supper. The three distinct layers are really pretty."

ROAST BEEF TORTILLA MELT

Honorable Mention, 1998

1/3 cup tomato salsa (as spicy as you like it)

3 tablespoons mayonnaise

3 thinly sliced green onions

2 tablespoons chopped cilantro

4 six-inch flour tortillas

4 large, thin slices roast beef

1 package (6 ounces) sliced Monterey Jack cheese

1 ripe avocado, sliced

Heat broiler. Combine salsa, mayonnaise, green onions, and cilantro. Place tortillas on baking sheet (one that fits in broiler). Reserve 4 tablespoons salsa mixture; spread remainder over tortillas. Top with roast beef and cheese slices. Broil until cheese browns lightly, 1 to 3 minutes. Top with avocado and remaining salsa mixture. Cut tortillas in quarters; serve immediately.

Makes 4 to 5 servings.

WOLFGANG H. M. HANAU, WEST PALM BEACH, FLORIDA

SMOKED WHITEFISH, CUCUMBER, AND DILL SPREAD

Peel cucumber, cut it in half lengthwise, and scoop out seeds. Finely chop the cucumber flesh, then combine with cream cheese, green onion, chopped dill, and freshly ground black pepper to taste. Carefully skin and bone the smoked whitefish, then "flake" it with your fingers or a fork and make sure all the bones are removed. Fold whitefish into the cream cheese mixture. Stir in fresh lemon juice to taste, if desired. Spread on your choice of bread or crackers.

Makes about 1 ½ cups of spread.

½ medium cucumber

1 package (8 ounces) cream cheese, softened

2 tablespoons minced green onion

2 to 3 teaspoons chopped fresh dill

freshly ground black pepper

½ pound smoked whitefish

1 to 2 tablespoons fresh lemon juice (optional)

cocktail rye bread, sliced sourdough French baguette, or sesame crackers

KEN SCHWEBS, SUN PRAIRIE, WISCONSIN

"This recipe is the one I've received the most compliments on in all my 75 years."

LOCAL FLAVOR

For lovers of heartland cuisine, the move toward American regionalism has been one of the most gratifying trends to come along in decades in the culinary world. At first, foods from Cajun country and the Southwest got all the attention, but these days ingredients like Door County tart cherries and Wisconsin aged cheddar, and specialties like grilled bratwurst and Milwaukee microbrews, are also acclaimed. Encouraged, restaurant chefs feature more and more local crops and products on their menus, and home cooks are following suit. They go beyond the obvious—like cheese, beer, and sausage—and add many lesser known, but just as distinctive, Wisconsin-produced items to their repertoire, including:

- Honey
- Cranberries
- Ginseng
- Horseradish
- Lingonberries
- Whitefish caviar
- Smoked whitefish and chubs
- Farm-raised trout
- Bison
- Maple syrup products
- Catfish
- Wild rice
- Turkey
- Dried cherries and cherry cider
- Goat and sheep milk cheeses
- Crayfish
- Heirloom apples
- Morel mushrooms
- Popcorn

MUSHROOM AND CHEESE-STUFFED VIENNA BREAD

Honorable Mention, 1997

Heat oven to 350 degrees. Using a sharp serrated knife and without cutting all the way to the bottom of the loaf, make 2-inch slices from the top of loaf, first lengthwise then crosswise. The loaf will be cut with cubelike sections when you've finished slicing both ways. Stuff with layers of mushrooms and cheese, gently pressing each layer towards bottom of loaf. Place on double thickness of aluminum foil. Melt butter with remaining ingredients; drizzle this into the stuffed cuts of the bread. Wrap loaf tightly in the foil; bake 35 to 40 minutes. Serve warm. Guests can break off pieces to eat with their fingers.

Makes 10 servings.

1 large unsliced loaf Vienna-style bread

12 ounces white or brown mushrooms, sliced (about 6 cups)

12 ounces shredded Swiss cheese (about 3 cups)

1/2 cup (1 stick) butter

1 teaspoon minced garlic

2 tablespoons finely chopped onion

1 to 2 tablespoons poppy seeds

1 teaspoon seasoned salt

1 teaspoon dry mustard

1 teaspoon fresh lemon juice

CHRISTINE KLESSIG, AMHERST JUNCTION, WISCONSIN

"Stuffed bread can also be baked on a Weber-type grill, using the indirect heat method."

ALLSPICED-UP APPLE DIP

1 package (8 ounces) cream cheese, softened

1/2 cup sour cream

2 tablespoons frozen orange juice concentrate, thawed

2 tablespoons honey

1/2 teaspoon ground allspice

1/2 teaspoon grated orange zest (grate only outermost, orange part of the rind)

1 large tart apple

2 tablespoons finely chopped walnuts

1 tablespoon dried cranberries or dried cherries, chopped

1 tablespoon chopped fresh parsley

sliced apples for dipping (use a tasty Wisconsin variety, such as Lodi, Ida Red, Melba, Northern Spy, Snow, or Golden Russet)

Beat cream cheese and sour cream in mixing bowl until smooth. Beat in orange juice concentrate, honey, allspice, and orange zest. Peel and grate the apple; stir grated apple, walnuts, and dried fruit into the cream cheese mixture. Transfer to an attractive serving bowl; chill. To serve, garnish with chopped fresh parsley and surround with sliced apples for dipping. (To prevent the apple slices from turning brown too quickly, dip them in water to which lemon juice has been added, then drain well.)

Makes 4 to 6 servings.

ROXANNE E. CHAN, ALBANY, CALIFORNIA

CHUNKY FRESH TOMATO SALSA

Mix all ingredients. Serve as a dip with tortilla chips, a topping for grilled chicken or fish, or a salad dressing. Salsa will keep in the refrigerator up to three weeks; it may also be frozen (drain thawed salsa before serving).

Makes 2 ½ to 3 cups.

4 large tomatoes, peeled* and finely chopped

½ cup finely chopped onions

½ cup finely chopped green pepper

minced jalapeño pepper to taste (use 1 to 4 whole peppers, according to your "heat" preference)

2 teaspoons minced garlic

1 can (6 ounces) tomato paste

2 tablespoons chopped fresh cilantro or parsley

2 tablespoons salad oil

1 tablespoon fresh lemon or lime juice

1 tablespoon cider vinegar

1 tablespoon sugar

1 teaspoon salt

½ teaspoon dried oregano

*To peel tomatoes, cut a shallow "X" in bottom of each and immerse them briefly in boiling water. Drain, cool briefly, and slip off skins.

ROSE MARY BLASCZYK, CALEDONIA, WISCONSIN

"I always use fresh, fresh vegetables from my garden . . . everybody just loves that fresh taste."

BROCCOLI CHEDDAR DIP

1 container (16 ounces) Wisconsin cheddar cheese spread

$1/2$ small onion, grated

1 can (10 $3/4$ ounces) cream of mushroom soup

1 pound broccoli, finely chopped (use florets and tender part of stalk only)

grilled or toasted French bread slices, crackers, or tortilla chips

Combine cheese spread, grated onion, and mushroom soup in double boiler. Stir over low heat until well blended. Stir in chopped broccoli and heat several more minutes. Serve with grilled or toasted French bread slices, crackers, or tortilla chips.

Makes 6 to 8 servings.

LONA KOWALSKI, TWO RIVERS, WISCONSIN

"Try to get broccoli from a farmers' market or home-grown for better flavor. This is very colorful and appetizing to the eye. My family loves this; I hope others will too."

EASY TACO DIP

Honorable Mention, 1997

Mix cream cheese, sour cream, and taco seasoning; spread on platter. Layer remaining ingredients over cheese spread. Chill. Serve with tortilla chips.

Makes 10 to 12 servings.

1 package (8 ounces) cream cheese, softened
1 cup sour cream
½ to 1 tablespoon packaged taco seasoning (or more to taste)
shredded lettuce
diced tomatoes
chopped green onion
shredded cheddar
diced black olives

Mary Guertin, Manitowoc, Wisconsin

CHILI-GLAZED PORK SATAY

Glaze
1 cup white wine vinegar
3/4 cup sugar
1 tablespoon orange marmalade
1/4 teaspoon crushed red pepper flakes

Satay
1 pound lean ground pork
1/2 cup cornbread crumbs
1 teaspoon minced garlic, mashed to a paste with fork or flat of knife
1 tablespoon white wine vinegar
1 tablespoon fresh lime juice
1/4 teaspoon ground cumin
1 jalapeño, seeded and minced

Garnish
chopped fresh cilantro or parsley

Heat broiler or prepare outdoor grill. Place all glaze ingredients in medium saucepan with ½ cup water. Bring to boil, lower heat, and simmer hard until sauce is thickened to syrup consistency. You should have one-third to one-half cup of glaze. Keep warm.

Combine satay ingredients in bowl; mix well. Divide mixture into 16 portions. Form each portion around an 8-inch skewer into an oblong shape that is about 6 inches long and ⅓-inch thick. Broil or grill meat about 6 inches from heat source 2 to 3 minutes; turn and continue to cook until done, 2 to 3 minutes longer. Arrange 4 skewers on each of 4 plates. Drizzle glaze over meat. Sprinkle with chopped cilantro or parsley.

Makes 4 servings.

Roxanne E. Chan, Albany, California

MELON MOTIVATION

Frigid temperatures make for big appetites and Wisconsin is famous for both. But not during the dog days of August, when we endure another kind of torment: sticky, sweltering weather and the hunger for something cool and light. As author Molly O'Neill has written, "The summer appetite is like an indecisive lover. It is loath to commit to a full meal, looking to be convinced."

Melons convince us. Smiling wedges of honey-flavored cantaloupe. Fragrant, soft-fleshed muskmelon and spicy, mint-green honeydew. Crispy slabs of scarlet watermelon. Unresponsive appetites are no match for the likes of these seductive fruits. No matter how hot the day, how wilted the cook, melons make for cool and easy inspiration.

- Make a fruit salsa with chopped cantaloupe, green onion, hot peppers, and cilantro.
- Wrap super-thin slices of ham around honeydew wedges.
- Sauté firm wedges of cantaloupe with curry spices and serve as an appetizer or side dish.
- Cut several kinds of melons into large cubes and store in plastic tubs for easy snacking.
- Purée watermelon and mix with sugar and lemon for a vivid batch of liquid rejuvenation.
- Stir low-fat yogurt, honey, chopped fresh mint, and cantaloupe chunks into liquefied melon for a chilled soup.
- Cut softball-size muskmelons in half and fill the center with blueberries and cottage cheese, yogurt, or ice cream.

BRIE AND CRANBERRY CHUTNEY MELT

Chutney

1 cup fresh (or frozen and thawed) cranberries

3 tablespoons orange juice

1/2 cup sugar

1 small tart apple, peeled and finely chopped

1/4 cup finely chopped celery

1/4 teaspoon ground ginger

1/8 teaspoon ground cloves

1 1/2 teaspoons grated orange zest (grate outermost, orange part of rind only)

1/2 cup golden raisins or dried cranberries

Other ingredients

1 (8-ounce) round of brie

cooked, crumbled bacon (optional)

plain crackers

To make chutney: Combine cranberries, orange juice, and sugar in saucepan. Bring to simmer, stirring, and cook until cranberries soften, 5 to 10 minutes. Stir in remaining chutney ingredients. Cool. Cover and chill until ready to use.

To serve: Carefully slice rind from top of cheese round, removing only 1/8-inch from top. Place cheese round on large heatproof plate. Spoon 6 or more tablespoons chutney over cheese. Sprinkle with bacon, if desired. Heat in microwave or oven until cheese is softened but still retains its shape. Serve with crackers for dipping. (Remaining chutney can be used with meats and cheeses.)

Makes 6 to 8 servings.

CATHY A. WIRTZ, PRESQUE ISLE, WISCONSIN

OPEN-FACE CHICKEN, OLIVE, AND CHEESE SANDWICHES

Mix chicken and mayonnaise in bowl. Season with salt and pepper to taste. Toast bread on one side in broiler until light brown. Spread chicken mixture on untoasted side of each slice of bread and cover with a slice of cheese. Broil until cheese melts, 3 to 4 minutes. Garnish with sliced olives and serve immediately. Cut into quarters for an appetizer or serve whole as an open-face sandwich.

Makes 6 servings.

1 cup finely chopped cooked chicken

1/3 cup mayonnaise

salt and freshly ground black pepper

6 slices firm white bread (remove the crusts, if desired)

6 slices cheddar (slightly smaller than the bread slices)

1/3 cup stuffed green olives, sliced

ROBERT GRAY, ONALASKA, WISCONSIN

WISCONSIN CRANBERRY BRANDY SLUSH

1 small package
(3 ounces) raspberry-
flavored gelatin
1 cup boiling water
3 cups cold water
2 cups cranberry juice
1 can (12 ounces) orange
juice concentrate
1 can (12 ounces)
lemonade
concentrate
2 cups brandy
sweet soda (such as 7-Up
or Sprite) or sour soda
(such as 50-50)
orange slices and
maraschino cherries
for garnish

Place gelatin in large bowl; stir in boiling water until gelatin is completely dissolved. Stir in cold water, cranberry juice, orange juice and lemonade concentrates, and brandy. Stir until frozen concentrates are completely dissolved. Place mixture in freezer for several hours. To serve, spoon frozen slush into glasses, about one-half to three-quarters full. Add soda to fill glasses and garnish with orange slices and cherries.

Makes 16 to 24 servings.

Barbara Beilke, Tomahawk, Wisconsin

ROAST POTATO AND CAULIFLOWER SOUP

Heat oven to 400 degrees. Grease a large baking pan or line it with parchment paper or aluminum foil. Mix cauliflower, potatoes, garlic, cloves, and olive oil in bowl. Season to taste with salt and pepper. Spread in single layer in prepared pan. Roast until golden, stirring occasionally, 20 to 30 minutes.

Bring stock to simmer in soup pot. Add potato mixture and dried thyme; simmer until vegetables are tender, about 20 minutes. (If you're using fresh thyme, add it after soup has simmered 10 minutes.) Mash vegetables against sides of pot with large spoon or with hand-held potato masher. Stir in half-and-half; heat through. Stir in additional salt and pepper to taste, if desired.

Makes 4 servings.

2 cups cauliflower florets (in bite-size pieces)

2 cups peeled, cubed potatoes

2 to 4 garlic cloves, peeled

2 tablespoons olive oil

salt and freshly ground black pepper

4 cups chicken or vegetable stock

$1/2$ teaspoon dried thyme or 2 to 3 teaspoons chopped fresh thyme

$1/2$ cup half-and-half

ANNE MEANS, MADISON, WISCONSIN

PORTOBELLO BEEF AND BARLEY SOUP

1 pound extra lean
    ground beef
olive oil (if needed)
1 large onion, chopped
10 ounces Portobello
    mushrooms, sliced
    (5 to 6 cups)
5 to 6 cups beef broth,
    divided
1/2 cup pearl barley or
    quick barley
1 tablespoon chopped
    fresh tarragon or
    1 teaspoon dried
1/2 cup half-and-half
salt and freshly ground
    black pepper
fresh tarragon sprigs or
    chopped fresh
    tarragon

Brown meat over high heat in large, heavy skillet, breaking up beef into chunks as it browns. Transfer meat to a soup pot. Reduce heat under skillet to medium-high and if skillet is dry of fat, add a little olive oil to it. Add onions and mushrooms; saute, stirring often, until vegetables are barely tender and mushrooms have given up their liquid, 5 to 10 minutes. Add cooked vegetables to soup pot. Stir in 5 cups broth, pearl barley, and tarragon. Bring to simmer, cover, and cook over low heat until barley is tender, 30 to 40 minutes. (It will take less time if you use quick barley.) Stir in half-and-half and any remaining beef broth to reach desired consistency; heat through. Season with salt and pepper to taste. Ladle into bowls and garnish with tarragon sprigs or chopped fresh tarragon.

Makes 4 to 6 servings.

LISA KEYS, MIDDLEBURY, CONNECTICUT

CREAMY LEEK AND POTATO SOUP WITH FRESH HERBS

Cut off and discard deep green parts of leeks, leaving only the white and pale green portions. Cut them in half lengthwise and slice thinly. Place in colander and rinse under cold water to remove any dirt; drain well.

Melt butter in large, heavy saucepan over medium heat. Stir in leeks, cover, and cook, stirring occasionally, until nearly tender, about 10 minutes. Meanwhile, peel and dice potatoes. When leeks are nearly tender, add potatoes and chicken stock. Bring to simmer, cover, and cook 10 minutes. Stir in herbs and continue to simmer until vegetables are tender, 5 to 8 minutes longer. Remove from heat.

In a food processor or blender, purée half or more of the vegetables, depending on how creamy or chunky you'd like the soup. Return purée to saucepan; stir in half-and-half. Add salt and pepper to taste. Simmer briefly to heat through. Garnish each bowl with chopped fresh herbs or herb sprig.

Makes 6 to 8 servings.

4 medium leeks

4 tablespoons butter

2 pounds Russet potatoes

3 ½ cups homemade chicken stock or low-salt canned chicken broth

3 tablespoons chopped fresh herbs (use two or more of the following: parsley, thyme, chives, dill, lemon balm, marjoram)

1 cup half-and-half*

salt and freshly ground black pepper

additional chopped fresh herbs or herb sprigs

*For a lower-fat soup, substitute more chicken broth for the half-and-half.

HOLLY SLUSSER, OREGON, WISCONSIN

"If you want a creamy soup, purée all of it, but I like chunks of leek and potato in mine. Serve with warm bread—yum!"

BACK TO WHERE WE ONCE BELONGED

There was a time, in the not too distant past, when chemical pesticides, irradiation, and biotechnology did not exist. Neither did the phrase "organic food," for that matter, because virtually all food was raised naturally.

Pesticides ruled agriculture for several decades but things are changing now. After a brief stint as a hippie-influenced alternative crusade, then a quick spell as a foodie fad, the organic movement is coming into its own. "The reasons to support organic agriculture have become increasingly familiar," wrote Elaine Lipson in a 1998 *Delicious!* magazine article. "Organic farming protects the water supply, enriches the soil, encourages biodiversity, and helps reduce the toxic burden on our bodies. By buying organic food, we offer organic farmers a lifeline."

Resources abound; here are a few:

- Healthy Meats! This Madison-area farmers group direct-markets free-range pastured chicken and sustainably raised beef, lamb, pork, and poultry. For more infomation, call the Michael Fields Agricultural Institute, 414-642-3303.
- Community Supported Agriculture. To secure a season's worth of organic produce, buy a share of the harvest. For a directory of upper Midwest subscription farms call the Michael Fields Agricultural Institute, 414-642-3303.
- *The Green Kitchen Handbook,* by Annie Berthold-Bond (HarperPerennial, 1997). Practical advice, references, and sources.
- U.S. Food Cooperative Directory. For a list of cooperatives by state, go to the Web site at www.prairienet.org/co-op/directory/.

SAUSAGE CORN CHOWDER

Heat large skillet over medium-high flame. Add sausage and onions; cook, tossing often, until pork is lightly browned and onions are nearly tender, about 10 minutes. Remove sausage and onions from pan with slotted spoon, drain on paper towels, then transfer to soup pot.

Add potatoes, chicken broth, and herbs to pot. Bring to low simmer, cover, and cook until potatoes are tender, about 15 minutes. Stir in corn and milk; simmer 3 to 5 minutes. Add salt and pepper to taste.

Makes 6 servings.

1 pound bulk pork sausage or mild Italian sausage
1 cup chopped onion
2 to 3 cups peeled, cubed potatoes
2 $1/2$ cups chicken broth
1 tablespoon chopped fresh rosemary or basil, or 1 teaspoon dried
1 tablespoon chopped fresh marjoram, or 1 teaspoon dried
2 cups corn kernels
2 $1/2$ to 3 cups whole milk
salt and freshly ground black pepper

ADAPTED FROM A RECIPE BY JOYCE PHENICIE, HARTLAND, WISCONSIN

SWEET POTATO SOUP

2 tablespoons olive oil

1 cup chopped onion

1 to 2 teaspoons minced garlic

6 cups chicken or vegetable broth

2 pounds sweet potatoes, peeled and diced (about 5 cups)

1 pound Russet potatoes, peeled and diced (2 to 3 cups)

½ cup chopped carrots

½ cup chopped celery

1 teaspoon dried thyme

salt and freshly ground black pepper to taste

chopped fresh chives

Heat olive oil in soup pot over medium flame. Add onion and garlic; cook, stirring occasionally, 4 to 5 minutes. Add broth, sweet potatoes, Russets, carrots, celery, and thyme. Bring to simmer, reduce heat to low, and cook until vegetables are very tender, about 15 minutes. Season to taste with salt and pepper.

The soup is very good as is, but even better if you mash some of the potatoes against the sides of the pot to thicken the liquid. It's best of all when you purée some or all of the solids in a food processor or blender, then recombine the purée with the liquid. Garnish each bowl with chopped chives.

Makes 4 to 6 servings.

DARLA LANGE, DOUSMAN, WISCONSIN

"Serve with tossed salad and hot bread or rolls to complete the meal."

SWISS CREAM OF POTATO SOUP

Peel potatoes, place in a heavy pot with water to cover, bring to boil, and cook until tender. Meanwhile, dice the bacon and fry it in a skillet with the onions. When potatoes are done, drain them and return them to the pot. Cook over low heat to "dry" them briefly. Mash the potatoes with a little of the milk. Add the bacon–onion mixture, parsley, nutmeg, mustard, and 1 teaspoon salt. Stir in the remaining milk. Bring to simmer over low heat, stirring often. Season to taste with white pepper and additional salt, if needed. Sprinkle each serving with grated Swiss cheese.

Makes 4 servings.

4 medium potatoes (approximately 1 ¾ pounds)

2 thick slices bacon

⅓ cup finely chopped onion

3 cups milk, divided

1 tablespoon minced fresh parsley

½ teaspoon nutmeg

¼ teaspoon dried mustard

1 or more teaspoons salt

ground white pepper

grated Swiss cheese (aged or mild)

MARGARET ZICKERT, DEERFIELD, WISCONSIN

RIP'S POLISH SAUSAGE AND CABBAGE CHOWDER

2 tablespoons butter or olive oil

1 ½ cups cubed rutabaga

1 cup chopped onion

3 cups cubed red potatoes

½ small head cabbage, thickly shredded

1 ½ cups chopped carrots

5 cups chicken broth (approx.)

1 pound Polish sausage, cut into small chunks

1 can (10 ¾ ounces) cream of chicken soup

1 to 2 teaspoons dried dill

1 cup milk

salt and freshly ground black pepper

3 tablespoons flour (optional)

Melt butter or heat olive oil in soup pot over medium-low heat. Add rutabaga and onions; cook, stirring, 3 to 5 minutes. Add potatoes, cabbage, carrots, and enough chicken broth to cover vegetables. Bring to simmer and cook until vegetables are nearly tender. Stir in Polish sausage, cream of chicken soup, dill, milk, and salt and pepper to taste. Simmer 10 minutes longer. If you want to thicken the soup, whisk the flour with ¼ cup water (or shake flour and water in a lidded jar) and add to the simmering soup.

Makes 8 servings.

ADAPTED FROM A RECIPE BY PATRICIA WILLIAMS, REWEY, WISCONSIN

"It's easy to make a larger batch by putting in more of everything, depending on how many you want to serve. It's always excellent the next day after things sit together."

HEARTY PORK AND WILD RICE SOUP

Trim and cube pork steak. Dredge in flour and shake off the excess. Heat oil in skillet over medium-high flame. Add meat in batches to brown it, transferring each batch to a soup pot or Dutch oven. Lower heat, add garlic to skillet, and cook gently 2 to 3 minutes. Stir in some of the stock to loosen any bits on bottom of skillet. Add contents of the skillet to the meat along with remaining stock, Worcestershire sauce, mustard, bay leaf, and thyme. Bring to simmer, cover, and cook gently over low heat 20 minutes.

Add wild rice (and barley, if using), cover again, and simmer gently 20 to 30 minutes. Stir in onion, carrots, and mushrooms; continue to simmer until vegetables are tender, about 15 minutes. Season with salt and pepper to taste.

Makes about 8 servings.

1 1/2 pounds lean pork steak
1/4 cup flour, seasoned
1 tablespoon vegetable oil
2 teaspoons minced garlic
9 cups beef or chicken stock, or use part stock and part water
1 tablespoon Worcestershire sauce
1 teaspoon brown mustard
1 bay leaf
1 teaspoon dried thyme
1 cup wild rice, or use 1/2 cup wild rice and 1/2 cup pearled barley
1 cup chopped onion
1 cup chopped carrots
1 cup sliced mushrooms
salt and freshly ground black pepper

SHELLY PLATTEN, AMHERST, WISCONSIN

2

SALADS and SIDE DISHES

Soup soothes and appetizers welcome but it is the salad course that brings out our creative side. The sheer magnitude of ingredient possibilities—vegetables, fruits, pastas, grains, dairy products, meat, fish, pantry staples—will inspire any cook, no matter how busy or inexperienced he or she may be.

Salads—and side dishes, too—are like the back-up musicians in a band: they complement the star performer, supplying a background riff that gives a meal depth and character. And like a talented guitarist giving an impressive solo, a side dish or salad can even outshine the main event. Some, such as the mixed green salad accented with grilled pork and fresh peaches in this chapter, are substantial and entertaining enough to gain main dish status in their own right.

When company is coming, we generally stick to the tried-and-true: an easy centerpiece roast or grilled meat, those lemon bars that have long been a favorite. But unlike the main course and dessert, salads are a sideshow. And since they're not the center of attention, the pressure is off. We're free to let down our hair a bit. We might, for example, vary a classic Waldorf salad as one recipe contest winner did, making it lighter by adding fruit-flavored yogurt instead of mayonnaise, and giving it a regional twist with dried cherries in place of raisins.

This creative streak has an affable side, especially in the Midwest, where cooking and dining are typically more informal, less self-conscious than on the fad-driven coasts. Known for their sense of humor, Wisconsinites like to have fun with their food (witness the Cow Pie confection or the Cheesehead phenomenon). Indeed, Wisconsin folks will make a party of nearly any meal, whether they're layering a dish with green and gold ingredients to honor the Packers (see page 44), or gathering around a churning pot in Door County for the fiery spectacle of a "fish boil-over."

Home cooks nowadays are increasingly comfortable "playing with their food." Improvisation comes easier partly because cooking shows, culinary magazines, Web sites, classes, clubs, and all sorts of resources abound, stimulating our imagination and building the confidence it takes to create distinctive dishes.

Mothers of Invention

Wisconsinites may be even more practiced than others in the role of maverick cook. We draw from a heritage of considerable ethnic and agricultural diversity, for one thing. But we also have a long-standing reputation for innovation stemming from the Progressive Era, when forward thinkers updated everything from politics to the dairy industry. What's more, the Wisconsin Idea, which encouraged the use of government and university resources in the private sector, taught us to value and utilize such assets. In Wisconsin today, a cook's assets include not just TV cooking shows and glossy magazines, but University of Wisconsin Extension classes, culinary programs at technical colleges, even local cookbook clubs. No wonder so many fresh ideas are coming out of Wisconsin kitchens.

No wonder the salads and side dishes herein—from mashed potato salad to a rice casserole spiked with pepper jack cheese—reflect the skill, playfulness, and creativity of Wisconsin.

WISCONSIN WALDORF SALAD

Winner, 1997

Cut apples into ½-inch chunks; toss with lemon juice to prevent browning. Combine with dried cherries, celery, and yogurt. Chill. Just before serving, sprinkle with almonds and top with fruit garnish.

Makes 6 servings.

4 large apples (use both sweet and tart, if available, and do not peel them)

2 to 3 tablespoons fresh lemon juice

⅓ cup dried Door County cherries

2 to 3 stalks celery, sliced

1 cup fruit-flavored yogurt, or 1 cup plain yogurt mixed with maple syrup and cinnamon to taste

½ cup chopped toasted almonds*

fresh berries, sliced star fruit, or kiwi for garnish

*To toast almonds, spread on baking sheet; bake at 350°, tossing occasionally until lightly colored, 8 minutes or more.

ANN GALBRAITH MILLER, GREEN BAY, WISCONSIN

"All recipes evolve. I love crunchy things and liked the idea of a Waldorf salad. But mayonnaise is fattening and I don't like the way it tastes with apples. So why not yogurt? Cook what you like!"

MASHED POTATO SALAD

5 pounds Russet potatoes, peeled and cut into large chunks

6 hard-cooked eggs, chopped

1 cup chopped onion

1 cup sliced radishes

½ cup chopped celery

1 ½ to 2 cups bottled salad dressing or mayonnaise

salt and freshly ground black pepper to taste

prepared mustard (optional)

chopped fresh chives (optional)

½ cup shredded cheddar cheese

Boil potatoes in salted water until tender. Drain and mash in large bowl. Cool to warm temperature. Gently stir in eggs, onion, radishes, and celery. Fold in salad dressing or mayonnaise, salt, and pepper. If desired, fold in some mustard or chopped fresh chives, or both. Top with cheese.

Makes 8 to 12 servings.

PATRICIA WILLIAMS, REWEY, WISCONSIN

"Like fine wine, this salad only gets better with age, so make it a day in advance. Be sure to keep tabs on your second batch; the first batch feeds six to eight people, but once they've got a taste for it, your next batch won't go as far!"

PEANUT BUTTER NOODLES

Honorable Mention, 1997

Boil spaghetti in salted water until tender. Rinse briefly; drain. Mix peanut butter, hot water, soy sauce, vinegar, sesame oil, and chili oil in large bowl until smooth. Toss in spaghetti, adding sesame seeds a few at a time. Add broccoli and toss well.

Makes 3 to 4 servings.

8 ounces spaghetti

1/4 cup peanut butter

1/4 cup hot water

3 tablespoons soy sauce (Wisconsin-produced Kikkoman brand is recommended)

2 tablespoons rice vinegar

1 tablespoon dark sesame oil

1 teaspoon hot chili oil

2 stalks broccoli, cooked crisp-tender, chopped

toasted sesame seeds*

*To toast sesame seeds, place in a cast iron pan over medium heat, tossing often, until lightly colored, 3 to 5 minutes.

RITA MULLEN, MADISON, WISCONSIN

DIGGING IT

What makes a good cook? As often as not, it's a good garden. Despite the fast pace of contemporary living, vegetable gardening remains something of an addiction in Wisconsin—maybe that's one of the reasons we eat so well here.

The state's reputation for rich, hearty foods stems in part from an agricultural heritage that focuses on meats and dairy foods. But the other, lighter side of the story includes the bounty we produce in backyard plots: crisp, spring-green lettuce; plump tomatoes; sweet bell peppers; frisky herbs; beans that go "pop" in your mouth.

Gardens hold many satisfactions for us. Wholesome, flavor-packed foods, yes, but also the joy of feeling soil give way after months of its giving us the cold shoulder. The thrill of seeing tiny pale pea shoots respond to our beckoning care. The knowledge that we are producing, being useful, and being nurtured in return.

Here are some resources for nurturing your addiction:

- *The Wisconsin Garden Guide*, by Jerry Minnich (Prairie Oak Press, Third Edition, 1995)
- *Growing and Using Herbs in the Midwest*, by Rosemary Divock (Amherst Press, 1996)
- *The Garden Book for Wisconsin*, by Melinda Myers (Cool Springs Press, 1999)
- *The Wisconsin Gardener*, Wisconsin Public Television weekly program; Web site at www.wpt.org/garden
- Wisconsin Gardening and Commercial Horticulture News, UW-Extension Web site, www.uwex.edu/ces/sehort/
- Seed Savers Exchange catalogue (heirloom seeds and gardening supplies), 3076 North Winn Road, Decorah, IA 52101, 319-382-5990
- Seed Savers Garden Store, 1919 Monroe Street, Madison, WI 53711, 608-280-8149.

DRIED CRANBERRY BROCCOLI SALAD

Bring large pot of water to rolling boil; add broccoli stems, count to 20, then add florets. Count to 20 again, then drain and rinse well with cold water. Drain. Dry broccoli on towels. Combine in large bowl with red onion, dried cranberries, and sunflower seeds. Whisk dressing ingredients in small bowl until smooth. Toss with broccoli mixture and chill at least 1 hour in refrigerator. Serve salad sprinkled with crumbled bacon.

Makes 4 to 6 servings.

Salad

1 bunch (about 1 pound) broccoli, cut into bite-size pieces (keep stems separate from florets)

1/3 cup finely diced red onion

1/2 cup dried cranberries

1/4 cup sunflower seeds

1/4 pound crisply fried bacon, crumbled (for garnish)

Dressing

1/2 cup mayonnaise

2 tablespoons milk

1 tablespoon sugar

salt and freshly ground black pepper to taste

Cathy A. Wirtz, Presque Isle, Wisconsin

WILD RICE DRIED CRANBERRY SALAD

Salad

1 cup wild rice

2 teaspoons olive oil

1 cup coarsely chopped hickory nuts or walnuts

½ cup dried cranberries

¼ cup finely diced celery

¼ cup finely diced red onion

grated zest of 1 lemon (grate only outermost, yellow part of the rind)

1 medium tart green apple

lettuce leaves

Dressing

2 tablespoons fresh lemon juice

2 tablespoons balsamic vinegar

4 tablespoons olive oil

salt

freshly ground pepper

Rinse wild rice. Place in medium saucepan with 2 cups water and 2 teaspoons olive oil. Cover, bring to boil, stir briefly, reduce to lowest simmer, and cover again. Cook over low heat until water is absorbed and rice is tender, 40 to 50 minutes. Uncover and let cool, stirring often, while you prepare the rest of the recipe.

Combine nuts, dried cranberries, celery, red onion, and lemon zest in bowl. Core and finely dice apple; stir into dried cranberry mixture. For dressing, combine lemon juice, vinegar, olive oil, and salt and pepper to taste in jar. Attach lid and shake vigorously. Toss dried cranberry mixture with half the dressing.

When rice has cooled to warm or room temperature, toss it with remaining dressing and dried cranberry mixture. Season with additional salt and pepper to taste. Let stand at room temperature, tossing occasionally, about 1 hour. Serve on lettuce leaves.

Makes 6 servings.

CATHY A. WIRTZ, PRESQUE ISLE, WISCONSIN

NORTH OF THE BORDER POTATO SALAD

Boil potatoes in salted water until barely tender; drain. Meanwhile, whisk dressing ingredients in large bowl. Prepare other ingredients. Toss all ingredients with dressing while potatoes are still warm. Let stand at room temperature ½ hour before serving.

Makes 8 servings.

2 pounds red potatoes, scrubbed

Dressing

½ cup olive oil

¼ cup cider vinegar

2 tablespoons sugar

2 tablespoons chili powder

1 teaspoon salt

2 or more dashes bottled hot pepper sauce

Other Ingredients

2 cups cooked corn kernels

1 small onion, finely diced

½ each green, yellow, and red bell pepper, diced (or substitute diced jícama for some of the bell peppers)

½ cup pitted, sliced black olives

¼ cup chopped fresh cilantro or parsley (optional)

VICKI DUEMLER, BRODHEAD, WISCONSIN

"This is a great salad for potlucks or picnics—there's no mayonnaise to spoil and it's different from other potato salads."

NEW AGE ROAST POTATO SALAD

6 cups thickly sliced Russet potatoes (unpeeled)

1/2 pound bacon, cooked crisp, drained, and broken into pieces

2 hard-cooked eggs, chopped

1/4 cup thinly sliced green onions

1 cup chopped green beans, blanched briefly in boiling water, drained

1 cup mayonnaise

salt and freshly ground black pepper to taste

Heat oven to 425 degrees. Oil a large baking sheet or spray it with cooking spray. Spread potatoes on the pan and roast until tender, about 35 minutes. Mix remaining ingredients with roasted potatoes while they are still warm. Serve salad warm or chilled. Fresh parsley or other herbs make a pretty garnish; you may also add some chopped herbs to the salad, if desired.

Makes 6 to 8 servings.

Marilyn Clay, Palatine, Illinois

BARBECUED PORK AND PEACH SALAD

Heat oven to 325 degrees. Fold narrow end of each tenderloin over and secure it with a toothpick to the meat (this will allow meat to cook evenly). Place tenderloins on wire rack in a shallow pan and sprinkle salt over the meat. Roast 35 minutes.

Meanwhile, make a barbecue sauce: Combine the ketchup, brown sugar, vinegar, and chili powder in a small bowl. When pork has roasted 35 minutes, spread sauce over meat. Roast meat until internal temperature taken with an instant-read thermometer has reached 170 degrees, about 10 to 15 minutes longer. Remove meat from oven and cool to room temperature.

To prepare peanut dressing: Combine lemon juice, soy sauce, brown sugar, hot pepper sauce, and ⅔ cup water in a blender; blend until brown sugar dissolves. Add peanut butter and blend until smooth. Reserve.

Blanch the pea pods in boiling water 30 seconds, then immediately plunge them into ice water. Drain well; pat dry and reserve.

Just before serving, dip fresh peaches in boiling water, then immediately plunge them into ice water. Peel and thickly slice peaches. Toss them with lemon juice in a bowl. (If you are using canned peaches, drain them well before tossing with lemon juice.) Slice pork tenderloins diagonally. Arrange salad greens on a large serving platter or individual plates. Arrange sliced pork, pea pods, and peaches on the greens. Sprinkle salad with peanuts. Spoon on some of the dressing. Serve salad with remaining dressing in a bowl on the side.

Makes 6 to 8 servings.

Pork
2 small pork tenderloins (about 1 ¼ to 1 ½ pounds total)
¼ teaspoon salt
¼ cup ketchup
2 tablespoons firmly packed brown sugar
2 teaspoons cider vinegar
½ teaspoon chili powder (or more to taste)

Peanut dressing
1 tablespoon fresh lemon juice
1 ½ tablespoons soy sauce
1 tablespoon firmly packed brown sugar
½ teaspoon hot pepper sauce (or more to taste)
1 cup creamy peanut butter

Other ingredients
¼ pound sugar-snap peas, tips and strings removed (or substitute snow peas)
2 large ripe peaches (or equivalent in canned peaches)
2 teaspoons fresh lemon juice
6 to 8 cups mixed salad greens
¼ cup unsalted roasted peanuts

Diane Halferty, Tucson, Arizona

DRIED CRANBERRY COUSCOUS SALAD WITH GARBANZO BEANS AND ALMONDS

....

¾ cup couscous

1 (15 ounce) can garbanzo beans (chick-peas), rinsed and drained

½ cup dried cranberries

½ cup finely chopped celery

¼ cup chopped green onions

3 tablespoons white wine vinegar

1 tablespoon Dijon-style mustard

1 tablespoon olive oil

salt and freshly ground black pepper

½ cup toasted whole almonds*

*To toast almonds, see instructions on page 29.

Bring 1 cup water to boil in small saucepan. Stir in couscous. Cover, remove from heat, and let stand 5 minutes. Uncover and fluff grains with a fork. Cool couscous 10 minutes.

Toss couscous, garbanzo beans, dried cranberries, celery, and green onions in large bowl. In a small bowl, whisk vinegar, mustard, and olive oil. Season to taste with salt and pepper. Pour over couscous and toss lightly. Taste and season with more salt and pepper if necessary. Just before serving, toss in the almonds. Serve either at room temperature or chilled.

Makes 6 servings.

....

Christine Klessig, Amherst Junction, Wisconsin

CREAMY ITALIAN PASTA SALAD

Cook pasta in lots of boiling salted water until barely tender. Add the broccoli florets, count to 30, then drain the pasta and broccoli thoroughly. Toss with remaining ingredients. Chill before serving.

Makes 4 to 6 servings.

6 ounces rotini (spiral pasta)

3/4 cup broccoli florets

1/4 cup finely chopped tomato

1/4 cup finely chopped black olives

1/4 cup finely chopped onion

1/4 cup finely diced green pepper

1/2 to 3/4 cup creamy Italian dressing (preferably homemade)

salt and freshly ground black pepper to taste

MILLIE SPENCER, REEDSBURG, WISCONSIN

CHICKEN ALMOND SALAD WITH CRANBERRY CHUTNEY SAUCE

••

Cranberry Chutney Sauce

1 teaspoon olive oil

1 cup finely chopped onion

2 teaspoons minced garlic

2 cups fresh cranberries

1/4 cup apple juice or apple cider

4 teaspoons sugar

pinch of salt

1 tablespoon cider vinegar

1/4 teaspoon dried sage

1/8 teaspoon grated orange zest (grate only outermost, orange part of the rind)

3 tablespoons orange marmalade

Salad

3 cups chopped cooked chicken

2 stalks celery, chopped

2 tablespoons chopped onion

1 apple, peeled and chopped

3 tablespoons lemon juice

1/4 cup vegetable or olive oil

2 tablespoons chopped fresh parsley

1 tablespoon Dijon-style mustard

1 teaspoon grated orange zest

salt and freshly ground black pepper

1/2 cup toasted slivered almonds*

Garnishes

romaine lettuce leaves

additional toasted slivered almonds*

thin slices of orange

* To toast almonds, see instructions on page 29 (reduce cooking time to 5 minutes or more).

To make chutney sauce: Heat olive oil in small pan over medium-low flame. Add onion and garlic; cook, stirring often, until onion is tender. Add remaining chutney ingredients except the marmalade. Stir well, bring to simmer and cook, stirring often, until thickened. Stir in marmalade and simmer 3 minutes longer. Cool to room temperature. Chill sauce until ready to serve.

To make chicken salad: Combine all the salad ingredients except almonds. Chill salad until ready to serve. Stir in the almonds just before serving.

To serve, spread lettuce leaves on large platter. Spoon chicken salad over lettuce. Spoon some of the chutney sauce around the chicken. Garnish with additional almonds and orange slices.

Makes 4 to 6 servings.

••

Zita Wilensky, North Miami Beach, Florida

TOMATO DAZE

A tomato is a bold being, brazen-red with sleek, taut skin and the cool slap of acidic flavor. But underneath the sassiness is something else, something food writer Molly O'Neill describes as "the miracle of such a powerful, juicy universe being contained in such fragile, tentative housing."

Tomatoes *are* miracles, especially the ones we grow ourselves: the ones we tuck deep into the ground on a warm May morning, the ones we check anxiously after a June thunderstorm, the ones we tie up with torn strips of old T-shirts. The warm, ruby, perfectly ripe ones we can't wait for, but do.

After all our tending and waiting, we down platefuls of thick-sliced tomatoes dressed only with salt and pepper. A week or two later, we add a drizzle of olive oil and some minced red onion. Maybe a bit of basil. Then, in the weeks that follow, we get creative (see ideas below). Finally, unbelievably, we're satiated; we begin to can, to freeze, to give our little red miracles away.

Tomato Ways

- Finely dice tomatoes, avocado, cucumber, and green onion; toss with olive oil and red wine vinegar.
- Make a chunky fresh tomato salsa with minced hot peppers, red onion, lime juice, fresh parsley and cilantro.
- Toss tomato and zucchini chunks with stale, torn bread, feta cheese, cured olives, fresh herbs, olive oil, and vinegar.
- Make gazpacho with homemade tomato juice as a base, flavored with lemon juice, olive oil, fresh parsley, garlic, and hot pepper sauce. Stir in diced tomatoes, hard-cooked eggs, onions, and cucumbers. Top with croutons and parmesan cheese.
- Stuff a tomato with one of the following: cottage cheese, tabbouleh, or scrambled eggs.
- Dip thick, firm tomato slices in seasoned flour, then a beaten egg, then a mixture of fresh basil, pressed garlic, and bread crumbs. Sauté in olive oil until golden brown on both sides.

PENNE WITH BLUE CHEESE, BEANS, TOMATOES, AND OLIVES

....

3/4 pound penne or ziti (small tube-shaped pasta)

1/2 pound green beans, cut into bite-size pieces

3 to 5 cloves garlic, minced and mashed to a paste with fork or flat of knife

5 tablespoons coarsely chopped fresh basil

3 tablespoons olive oil

4 ounces crumbled blue cheese

1 1/2 cups pitted cured black olives

2 plum tomatoes, coarsely chopped

salt and freshly ground black pepper to taste

Cook pasta in lots of boiling salted water. When pasta is about three-fourths done, add the green beans and continue boiling until pasta is tender. Drain well. Toss pasta with remaining ingredients and serve immediately.

Makes 4 to 6 servings.

....

COLLEEN COURON SMITH, TRACY, CALIFORNIA

"This is a super dish. It has lots of flavors and textures and is easy to prepare. You can replace the blue cheese with feta cheese or gruyère. You can replace the green beans with broccoli or asparagus. I have also added artichoke hearts and baby corns, as well as cooked chicken or ham. There's lots of room for creativity!"

BEEFY CAESAR SALAD

To prepare beef: Combine vinegar, soy sauce, garlic, lime juice, and pepper in large, shallow dish. Lay the flank steak in the marinade, turning to coat. Cover dish and let steak marinate in the refrigerator, turning often, 4 to 8 hours or at room temperature 1 hour.

To make dressing: Mash garlic, anchovies, and pepper to taste with a fork. Place in a large bowl; whisk in the egg white, Worcestershire sauce, mustard, and lemon juice. Whisk in olive oil in a thin stream.

Rinse lettuce leaves. Dry thoroughly in towels or salad spinner. Tear or chop lettuce into large pieces (including the inner ribs). Chill until ready to serve.

Heat coals for outdoor grill. Grill the steak until medium rare, 5 to 8 minutes per side. Let stand at room temperature 10 minutes. Slice meat thinly at a slant against the grain. Toss lettuce with desired amount of dressing, parmesan cheese, and croutons. Divide onto individual plates. Garnish with sliced steak and tomato wedges. Add parmesan and pepper as desired.

Makes 4 to 6 large servings.

Beef

3 tablespoons red wine vinegar

4 tablespoons soy sauce

1 tablespoon minced garlic, mashed to a paste with fork or flat of knife

juice of 1 lime

1 teaspoon freshly ground pepper

1 to 1 $\frac{1}{4}$ pounds flank steak

Dressing

2 teaspoons minced garlic

3 anchovies

freshly ground black pepper

1 fresh egg white

2 teaspoons Worcestershire sauce

2 teaspoons Dijon-style mustard

juice of $\frac{1}{2}$ lemon

6 tablespoons olive oil or more to taste

Salad

1 large or 2 medium heads romaine lettuce

$\frac{1}{2}$ cup or more freshly grated parmesan cheese

1 to 2 cups seasoned croutons

tomato wedges

ADAPTED FROM A RECIPE BY MARK MEDDAUGH, NEW BERLIN, WISCONSIN

GREEN BAY PACKER POTATOES

Potato layer

3 pounds Russet
    potatoes, peeled

1 cup sour cream

2 tablespoons milk

2 tablespoons butter

salt and freshly ground
    black pepper to taste

Squash layer

1 ½ cups cooked,
    puréed squash or
    pumpkin, or 1 can
    (15 ounces) pumpkin

1 tablespoon melted
    butter

salt and freshly ground
    black pepper to taste

Spinach layer

1 pound fresh spinach,
    stemmed, or
    1 package
    (10 ounces) frozen,
    chopped spinach,
    thawed

1 egg

2 teaspoons grated
    onion

salt and pepper to taste

Optional

¼ cup grated sharp
    cheddar

For potato layer, boil potatoes in salted water until very tender; drain well and while hot, mash them with sour cream, milk, butter, salt, and pepper.

For squash layer, combine puréed squash or pumpkin with melted butter, salt, and pepper.

For spinach layer, clean the leaves in cold water; drain. While they are still damp, place them in pot over medium heat to "steam" until limp, about 5 minutes. Rinse, drain, and squeeze out excess liquid. (If you are using frozen, thawed spinach, do not cook it; simply drain it well and squeeze out excess liquid.) Coarsely chop the spinach and combine with egg, onion, salt, and pepper.

To assemble and bake: Heat oven to 350 degrees. Butter a deep, two-quart casserole or baking dish. Layer the ingredients in the following order, smoothing each layer with a spatula: ⅓ of the potatoes; all the squash; another ⅓ of potatoes; all the spinach; and the final ⅓ of potatoes. Bake until heated through, about 40 minutes. If desired, sprinkle on the grated cheddar during final 5 to 10 minutes of baking.

Makes 8 servings.

Janet Magsamen, Madison, Wisconsin

ROSEMARY ROASTED POTATOES

Heat oven to 400 degrees. Scrub potatoes but do not peel them. Cut into large, bite-size chunks. (If using baby red potatoes, you may need only to halve or quarter them.) Toss potatoes with remaining ingredients. Spread in single layer on baking sheet with sides or in large baking pan. (For easy clean-up, line the pan with aluminum foil or parchment paper first.) Place in oven and roast the potatoes, tossing them every 15 minutes, until golden and tender, about 45 minutes or longer.

Makes 4 servings.

2 pounds Yukon Gold or baby red potatoes
2 tablespoons olive oil
2 teaspoons minced garlic
2 to 3 teaspoons dried rosemary, crumbled
1 teaspoon seasoning salt
freshly ground black pepper to taste

CHRISTINE KLESSIG, AMHERST JUNCTION, WISCONSIN

MUSHROOM PARMESAN BAKE

Honorable Mention, 1997

1 pound white or brown mushrooms, sliced (4 to 5 cups total)

2 tablespoons flour

1/4 cup chicken broth

1/2 cup half-and-half

freshly ground black pepper to taste

1/2 cup fine dry whole wheat bread crumbs

3/4 cup freshly grated parmesan cheese

4 tablespoons butter, cut into small pieces

Heat oven to 350 degrees. Place mushrooms in ungreased 2-quart baking dish. Whisk flour and chicken broth in small saucepan until smooth. Stir in half-and-half and pepper. Stir and cook over medium heat until thickened, about 3 minutes. Pour over mushrooms. Combine bread crumbs and parmesan; sprinkle over mushrooms. Dot with butter. Cover and bake until browned, about 30 minutes.

Makes 4 to 6 servings.

ROSE MARY BLASCZYK, CALEDONIA, WISCONSIN

POTATOES FANDANGO

Honorable Mention, 1998

Peel potatoes, or scrub them and pat dry. Cut thin slices crosswise into potatoes without cutting through bottom, so that potatoes can fan apart. Place in deep microwave-safe dish. Spoon melted butter over potatoes. Sprinkle with chopped herbs.

Cover dish and microwave on high power 5 minutes. Spoon melted butter over potatoes again, turn dish a quarter turn, and microwave 5 more minutes. Again spoon on the butter. Sprinkle each potato with 2 tablespoons parmesan, turn dish, and microwave 3 minutes. Turn dish, microwave until tender, 3 to 5 minutes longer. Sprinkle potatoes with paprika and salt to taste.

Transfer potatoes to serving platter. Garnish with herb sprigs. Stir mustard and sour cream into butter-herb mixture in baking dish. Warm 15 to 30 seconds in microwave. Transfer sauce to small bowl; serve with potatoes.

Makes 4 servings.

4 large baking potatoes (6 to 8 ounces each)

4 tablespoons butter, melted

2 teaspoons each chopped fresh parsley, basil, and oregano

1/2 cup freshly grated parmesan cheese

1/2 teaspoon paprika

salt

fresh herb sprigs

1 teaspoon Dijon-style mustard

1 cup sour cream

MARCIA M. CURTIS, WINSLOW, INDIANA

AT EASE

Dining has gone casual. Today's home entertaining involves more barbecues and brunches and fewer multicourse, sit-down dinners than in years gone by. In house design, cramped kitchens and formal dining rooms have given way to large living spaces that combine cooking and dining, with work counters and stools to encourage togetherness and the sharing of tasks among guests and hosts. Even potlucks have lost their stodginess, with light-hearted salads replacing the baroque, warmed-over casseroles of yesteryear.

In Wisconsin we favor supper clubs and fish fries over white tablecloth establishments. As for nouvelle cuisine, those fussy, minuscule "sculptures" that grace the plates at upscale restaurants, well, they make us chuckle a bit. The craze for coffee, however, is another thing; we really warm to the conversational, community spirit at coffeehouses.

During summertime, being all too aware of how soon the snow will again fly, we go for picnics. A meal outdoors is by nature an easygoing affair. The season's first cookout will invariably involve grilled bratwurst and homemade potato salad, but by July, when temperatures soar, there's little energy for cooking. So we simply pick a theme and go shopping. Here are some suggestions to keep your next picnic as carefree as can be:

- Italian bread, Genoa salami, marinated olives, sliced tomatoes, and wine
- Tortilla chips, guacamole, soft-shell tacos, tropical fruit, and chocolate bars
- English Stilton cheese, multigrain bread, pickled onions, apples, and chutney
- Spring rolls, sliced cucumbers, Asian-style chicken wings, and honeydew melon
- Summer sausage, colby, crackers, dried cranberries, and maple sugar candies.

CRANBERRY COUSCOUS SIDE DISH

Melt butter in large skillet over medium heat. Add onion, garlic, and almonds; cook, stirring often, until onions are tender. Add chicken broth, bring to a boil, and stir in couscous, cranberries, marmalade, currants, and lemon juice. Cover, remove from heat, and let stand 10 minutes. Add the chopped mint and fluff mixture with a fork.

Makes 6 servings.

2 tablespoons butter

1/2 cup finely chopped onion

2 teaspoons minced garlic

1/3 cup slivered almonds

2 cups homemade chicken broth, or 1 can (14 1/2 ounces) low-salt chicken broth

1 1/2 cups (10 ounces) couscous

2 cups fresh cranberries

1/4 cup orange marmalade

1 tablespoon currants

1 tablespoon lemon juice

1/4 cup chopped mint leaves

ROXANNE E. CHAN, ALBANY, CALIFORNIA

WHIPPED POTATO SALSA BAKE

4 medium Yukon Gold or white potatoes

1 tablespoon vegetable oil

2 tablespoons finely chopped onion

2 tablespoons finely chopped green pepper

1/2 cup seeded, chopped tomatoes

1/2 cup chunky tomato salsa (mild, medium, or hot)

1 teaspoon chili powder

1 very small package (1 1/2 ounces) cream cheese, softened

1 egg, beaten

salt and freshly ground black pepper

1/2 cup shredded cheddar

3 green pepper rings (sliced from a whole pepper)

Peel and cut up potatoes; boil in salted water until tender. Meanwhile, heat oil in small skillet over medium-low heat. Add onion, chopped green pepper, and tomatoes; cook, stirring often, until tender. Set aside.

When potatoes are cooked, drain and return them to the pot. Heat briefly over low flame until they are dry. Mash the potatoes with electric beaters set at low speed, slowly adding the salsa and chili powder, until potatoes are moist and smooth. Beat in the cream cheese. Stir in the egg and reserved tomato mixture. Season to taste with salt and pepper. Oil or spray a 1-quart casserole dish. Spoon in the potato mixture. The dish can be refrigerated until ready to bake.

Heat oven to 400 degrees. Bake casserole until heated through, about 30 minutes. Sprinkle with cheese and top with green pepper rings. Continue baking until cheese is melted, about 5 minutes.

Makes 6 servings.

Maria Thompson, Franklin, Wisconsin

THE KING'S SPUDS

••

Cut potatoes into large chunks and cook in boiling water or in microwave until tender but still firm. Drain and place in large bowl. Add cabbage, onion, celery, ham, horseradish, and Curt's Cooking Spice; toss to mix. Heat 1 tablespoon of the butter in large, nonstick skillet over medium heat. Transfer potato mixture to skillet, pressing it down lightly. Sprinkle lightly with salt and pepper. Cover and cook until bottom is lightly browned, 10 to 15 minutes. Uncover and turn mixture with spatula, adding more butter if necessary. Cover and cook until other side is browned, 10 to 15 minutes. Season with additional salt and pepper, if needed.

Makes 4 to 6 servings.

4 medium potatoes
3 to 4 cups coarsely chopped cabbage
1 cup chopped onion
1 cup chopped celery
1/4 cup chopped ham
1 tablespoon prepared horseradish (or more to taste)
1 1/2 teaspoons Curt's Premium Blend Cooking Spice (or other bottled seasoning spice)
1 to 2 tablespoons butter
salt and freshly ground black pepper

••

NANCY F. RAFAL, BAILEYS HARBOR, WISCONSIN

"[As a main course, this dish] needs only a tossed salad to make a very satisfying meal."

KUGELIS (GRATED POTATO AND BACON "LOAF")

½ pound bacon, chopped

2 ½ cups chopped onions

1 tablespoon minced garlic

3 pounds red potatoes

1 large can (12 ounces) evaporated milk

8 eggs, lightly beaten

salt and freshly ground black pepper

sour cream

Fry bacon in large skillet over medium heat until brown and crispy; drain on paper towels. Remove all but 2 tablespoons of bacon fat from the pan, reserving both amounts. Add onions to bacon fat in pan and cook, stirring often, until nearly tender. Stir in the garlic and continue to cook until onions are tender. Remove from heat and reserve.

Heat oven to 350 degrees. Grease a 9-by-13-inch casserole or baking pan. Peel potatoes and grate them on large holes of hand grater into a large bowl; add evaporated milk to prevent potatoes from turning dark. Stir in bacon bits, onion mixture, and 4 tablespoons of the reserved bacon fat (if less than 4 tablespoons remain, substitute melted butter for the amount needed). Stir in eggs. Season to taste with salt and pepper. Spread mixture into prepared pan and bake uncovered until set and lightly browned, 45 to 60 minutes. Serve with sour cream.

Makes 8 to 12 servings.

JANET S. DAILY, CHICAGO, ILLINOIS

PEPPER JACK RICE

Heat oven to 350 degrees. Grease a small casserole dish. Combine all ingredients except ½ cup of the cheese in bowl. Spread into prepared dish. Sprinkle remaining cheese on top. Bake uncovered until heated through, 20 to 30 minutes.

Makes 4 to 6 servings.

2 cups cooked white or brown rice

1 small can (4 ounces) mild chile peppers, drained and diced

1 cup sour cream

2 cups shredded pepper jack cheese, divided

LISA DIMMITT-EVERY, WEST SALEM, WISCONSIN

"Only four ingredients—easy!"

SONORAN CORNMEAL CHEESE PANCAKES

1/2 cup yellow cornmeal

1/4 cup flour

1 1/2 teaspoons baking powder

3/4 cup milk

1 egg, beaten

1 tablespoon vegetable oil

3/4 cup shredded cheddar

1/2 to 1 small can (4 ounces) mild chili peppers, drained and diced

1 green onion, chopped

1/2 teaspoon dried oregano

salt and freshly ground black pepper to taste

bottled chunky salsa

Combine all ingredients except salsa in the order listed in a bowl. Heat a lightly oiled griddle or large, heavy skillet over medium-high heat. Pour or spoon 1/4 cup batter onto hot griddle for each pancake. Cook pancakes until bubbles appear on surface and edges look slightly dry. Flip pancakes and continue cooking until bottoms are light brown. Serve with salsa.

Makes 4 servings.

DIANE HALFERTY, TUCSON, ARIZONA

"Guacamole also goes well with this dish."

CHEDDAR CHEESE NOODLE PIE

Melt 1 tablespoon of the butter in medium skillet; add onion and cook, stirring often, until limp and translucent (do not let them brown). Meanwhile, cook noodles in lots of boiling salted water until tender; drain well. Set cooked onions and noodles aside. Heat oven to 375 degrees.

To make crust: Melt remaining butter in saucepan over medium heat; stir in flour. Cook gently, stirring, several minutes. Stir in 1 cup shredded cheese and the dry mustard until cheese melts. Cool mixture slightly and spread in bottom and up the sides of a 9-inch glass pie plate.

Beat eggs in medium bowl. Stir in reserved onions, reserved noodles, remaining 1 cup grated cheese, and hot milk. Season to taste with salt and pepper. Spread mixture in crust. Bake until top is lightly browned and pie is bubbly, 30 to 45 minutes. Let pie stand 5 to 10 minutes before serving.

Makes 6 to 8 servings.

6 tablespoons butter, divided
1 medium sweet onion, chopped
1 ½ cups wide egg noodles (approximately 2 ½ ounces)
scant ¾ cup flour
2 cups shredded cheddar, divided
1 teaspoon dry mustard
2 eggs
1 cup hot milk
salt and freshly ground black pepper

Lois Evensen, Amherst, Wisconsin

3

MAIN DISHES

Let's admit it. Wisconsinites are big eaters. With a cold climate and an agricultural heritage like ours, what would you expect? Sure, we're trying to watch the cholesterol and fat. Yes, we're working healthful foods like vegetables and whole grains into our diets. And of course we want the freshest, tastiest, most wholesome victuals we can find. But asked if we prefer quality or quantity, we're likely to request an order of each.

Liberal Leanings

We love main courses for their bounty. Like midwesterners themselves, a main dish has a generous nature. It's bigger than an appetizer. There's enough for everyone plus maybe seconds, and even leftovers, too. The main dish is the important part of a meal. It comes on a platter fringed with garnishes and served with side dishes, the culinary counterpart to a benevolent monarch carried on a gilded litter, surrounded by loyal subjects.

Entrées typically feature meat or fish. Beef stew, grilled bratwurst, roast pork, stuffed turkey, pan-fried perch, venison sausage—there's no denying the satisfactions of such fare. It's in our blood: Native peoples from the Great Lakes region hunted and fished. European settlers butchered and processed farm and wild animals. Today, the state's farmers raise everything from cattle and hogs to trout and buffalo.

Most cooks instinctively think of meat or fish for the main course, but are increasingly turning to vegetables, grains, and soy products to replace or supplement it. Concerned about health and the environment, they find fresh, flavorful new ways to cook light, to eat "right." Like the contributors in this section, they sometimes forego the deep-fried cod and prepare panfish layered with tomatoes, zucchini, onions, and fresh herbs. They may bake lean pork chops with chicken stock and barley or use Italian sausage to flavor a vegetable-rich ragout.

Heart and Soul Food

Whatever its ingredients—fish, fowl, vegetables, meat—the main course is the core, the heart-and-soul of a meal. So we cook it with "soul," putting something of ourselves, something of our ancestors, into it. We make it ethnic.

The strong cultural influence on Wisconsin cuisine stems first from the state's immigrant past. We can thank our forefathers from the 19th century for such main dish specialties as rouladen, lutefisk, and trippe (a Belgian pork and cabbage sausage), while more recent newcomers have given us pork tamales and Laotian laab (a meat-and-vegetable roll-up featured in this chapter). From Lake Michigan to the Mississippi River, from Bayfield to the Illinois border, there are innumerable pockets of ethnic settlement where people enjoy and celebrate traditional foods. In fact, some communities count certain dishes as part of their very identity: witness the bratwurst of Sheboygan and the Cornish pasty of Mineral Point.

While heritage foods play a role in our lives, a relatively new and very compelling global awareness also affects our entrées, indeed, our entire diet. In large towns, we frequent Middle Eastern restaurants and Japanese noodle houses. During travels abroad, we order Peruvian *cuy* (guinea pig) and sip Oaxacan *mezcal*. We learn how to prepare *burek* on the Food Network and read about innumerable variations of paella in food magazines. These days, dishes like pork stir-fry and Italian-style stuffed shells, both found in this chapter, are as familiar as beef roast and mashed potatoes. The Information Age keeps us up to date and keeps us expanding our culinary horizons.

Often, for inspiration, we go no further than the national borders. For American regional flavor we down Kansas City barbecue, New England clam chowder, and Tex-Mex nachos. There's an ethnic factor in these dishes, too, intermingled with regional foodstuffs and the personal touch of individual cooks.

Despite all the outside influences, the most satisfying foods are often those that come from close by. It is a Wisconsin diner's great good fortune to live near the source of world-class dairy products, meats from farm and field, seasonal crops, and an array of specialty products from maple syrup to microbrews. We've always known that "our" food tastes great, but now, encouraged by the culinary trend towards regional foods, and by a growing appreciation for buying locally and cooking seasonally, we're grasping the fact that brats and fish boils are as every bit as "legitimate," every bit as deserving of recognition and pride, as fajitas or filé gumbo.

We're like Dorothy in *The Wizard of Oz*: only by traveling far away have we come to realize there's no place like home.

BEER MUSTARD BRATS

Winner, 1997

Prick bratwurst all over. Combine remaining ingredients in large, sealable plastic bag. Add brats, seal, and place in bowl. Marinate brats in refrigerator 8 to 24 hours, turning bag occasionally. Drain and grill. Tuck into brat buns and enjoy with Wisconsin beer.

Makes 8 servings.

8 Wisconsin bratwurst

1 cup Wisconsin beer (LaVona uses Huber)

$1/4$ cup Dijon-style mustard

3 tablespoons molasses

2 teaspoons Worcestershire sauce

$1/2$ teaspoon nutmeg

$1/4$ teaspoon cloves

LaVona Quinn, McFarland, Wisconsin

"Everybody tells me I'm a good cook. But you have to be a good cook if you have eight children!"

NORTH WOODS PANFISH
AND HARVEST VEGETABLES

Honorable Mention, 1997

3 large potatoes, peeled and sliced thin

salt and freshly ground black pepper

1/2 pound mushrooms, sliced (2 to 3 cups)

1 to 2 small zucchini, sliced

4 large tomatoes, peeled,* seeded, and sliced

2 to 4 green onions, chopped

2 teaspoons each chopped fresh thyme, basil, and oregano, or 1/2 teaspoon of each dried, divided

1 1/2 pounds perch, blue gill, walleye, rainbow trout, or other fish fillets

2 to 3 tablespoons butter, melted

*To peel tomatoes, see instructions on page 9.

Heat oven to 350 degrees. Butter a large baking dish, add potatoes, and season with salt and pepper to taste. Cover with foil; bake 20 minutes. Uncover dish and layer mushrooms, zucchini, tomatoes, and green onions over partially cooked potatoes. Season lightly with salt, pepper, and half the herbs. Cover and continue to bake 10 minutes. Uncover dish and layer fish over vegetables; sprinkle on melted butter and remaining herbs; season lightly with salt and pepper. Bake uncovered 15 minutes, or until fish is tender and lightly browned.

Makes 6 to 8 servings.

KATHRYN GREFE, MAUSTON, WISCONSIN

GOURMET GRILLED STUFFED PORK CHOPS

Honorable Mention, 1997

For stuffing, mix all ingredients except pork chops in bowl. To make pockets for the stuffing, hold a chop in your hand with the bone against your palm. Insert a sharp, thin-bladed knife horizontally into the meat until it nearly touches the bone. Gently swing the blade back and forth horizontally to create a wide pocket within the meat while widening the opening to no more than 1 ½ inches. With fingers or small spoon, fill pocket with stuffing. (The chop will hold more than you think.) Secure the opening with a single toothpick. Repeat with remaining chops and stuffing. Refrigerate until ready to cook. Bring pork chops to room temperature before grilling.

Makes 4 servings.

1 can (13 ¾ ounces) artichoke hearts, drained and chopped

1 cup cooked, drained, and chopped fresh spinach leaves*

1 to 2 tablespoons minced garlic

2 green onions, chopped

6 large black olives, chopped

⅓ cup chopped walnuts

2 ounces blue cheese, crumbled

2 tablespoons freshly grated parmesan cheese

freshly ground black pepper to taste

4 large extra-thick pork chops

*For instructions, see page 44.

DOUGLAS A. GILBERTS, PLOVER, WISCONSIN

"If you end up with extra stuffing, you can heat it and serve it on top of the chops."

LINKS WITH THE PAST

One of the mid-game entertainments at Milwaukee Brewer events is the "Sausage Race." During each home game, four costumed characters—the Bratwurst, the Italian Sausage, the Polish Sausage, and the Hot Dog—sprint around the field in a good-natured fight to the finish. Meanwhile, in the stands, baseball fans munch on the runners' real-life, edible counterparts (supplied for Brewer games by a local company called Klement's). As the crowd cheers for the assortment of jogging sausages, I like to think they're also applauding what the sausages represent: the state's ethnic diversity.

From Swiss-style landjaeger to Mexican chorizo, sausage is our heritage. While we splurge on whole-link sandwiches at ball games, at home we let a little sausage go a long way in more healthful combinations. Here are a few possibilities:

- Boiled red potatoes, caraway-seasoned sauerkraut, cooked corn, and chunks of grilled turkey kielbasa
- Red cabbage braised with onions and vinegar, mounded on a platter and topped with pieces of pan-fried Swedish potato sausage
- Baked casserole of corkscrew pasta, chopped spinach leaves, crumbled Italian sausage, tomatoes, and feta cheese
- Chopped ring bologna or mettwurst sautéed with mixed winter greens and garlic
- Black beans over rice garnished with cooked, crumbled chorizo
- Thin rounds of smoked or cooked sausage added to an antipasto platter, vegetable soup, or almost any kind of salad: tossed greens, pasta, rice, bean, etc.

SAUSAGE RAGOUT

Winner, 1998

Heat large, heavy Dutch oven or deep braising pan over medium heat. Add bacon and cook until bacon begins to brown. Stir in all the seasonings except fresh parsley. Stir in onions, peppers, potatoes, and sausage. Cook, stirring often, until potatoes are barely tender, 20 to 25 minutes. Stir in zucchini and tomatoes. Cover and cook, stirring often, until zucchini is barely tender, about 10 minutes. Sprinkle with fresh parsley and serve with sour cream.

Makes 6 to 8 servings.

1/2 pound thick-cut bacon, chopped

1 1/2 teaspoons paprika (sweet or hot, according to your preference)

1 teaspoon each dried marjoram, oregano, and caraway seed

1/2 teaspoon crushed red pepper flakes (or more to taste)

1 bay leaf

salt and freshly ground black pepper to taste

2 large onions, chopped

2 large green peppers, chopped

1 large sweet red pepper, chopped

2 medium potatoes, unpeeled, cut into 1/2-inch slices

1 pound knockwurst or other smoked sausage, cut into 1/2-inch slices

2 medium zucchini, cut into 1/2-inch slices

2 medium tomatoes, chopped

2 tablespoons chopped fresh parsley

sour cream

VICKI DUEMLER, BRODHEAD, WISCONSIN

"This is great in the late summer and early fall when gardens are full. It's delicious with hearty rye bread spread with sweet butter."

APPLE SPICED BEEF ROAST

Winner, 1998

1/4 cup soy sauce

1/4 cup tomato salsa

1/4 cup frozen apple juice concentrate, thawed

1/4 cup dry sherry

2 teaspoons pumpkin pie spice

2 teaspoons minced garlic

3 pounds boneless beef rump roast

2 cups sweet red pepper chunks

3 cups unpeeled Granny Smith apple chunks

2 tablespoons toasted pine nuts for garnish

Mix soy sauce, salsa, apple juice concentrate, sherry, pumpkin pie spice, garlic, and 4 cups water in Dutch oven or deep electric frying pan. Bring to boil, add beef roast, reduce heat to very low (or set electric pan to 250 degrees), and simmer until beef is tender, 1 to 2 hours.

Remove roast; keep warm. Raise heat; boil until liquid is reduced to 1 cup. Reserve 1/4 cup of the liquid. Add sweet peppers and apples to remaining 3/4 cup liquid; cook over high heat, stirring often, until liquid is mostly evaporated, about 3 minutes.

Slice beef; arrange on platter. Spoon reserved liquid over beef. Surround with sweet pepper mixture. Sprinkle with pine nuts.

Makes 8 servings.

LOANNE CHIU, FORT WORTH, TEXAS

Born in Indonesia, land of the Spice Islands, Loanne Chiu says, "I literally grew up with spices. It has always struck me how people in the United States and Europe use certain spices only for baking. I made this recipe to show how spices can be used differently."

FARMHOUSE CHEDDAR-TOPPED CHICKEN AND APPLE SAUTÉ

Winner, 1998

Combine butter, red onions, maple syrup, ¼ cup cider, and ½ teaspoon salt in large nonstick skillet over medium-low heat. Cover and cook 15 minutes, stirring often. Uncover, raise heat to medium, and cook 15 minutes longer. Stir in apples and ¼ cup cider; raise heat to high and cook, stirring often, until apples are softened, onions have darkened, and nearly all the liquid has reduced.

Meanwhile, heat vegetable oil in large nonstick skillet over medium-high heat. Add chicken, season with salt and pepper to taste, and sauté until golden brown, 2 to 3 minutes per side. Add remaining ½ cup cider and the thyme. Simmer until cider is reduced to a glaze, 5 to 10 minutes.

Heat broiler. Place chicken thighs in flameproof baking dish. Spoon glaze over chicken. Top each thigh with onion-apple mixture and cheddar. Broil until cheese melts, 1 to 2 minutes.

Makes 4 to 8 servings.

2 tablespoons butter
3 medium red onions, very thinly sliced
¼ cup pure maple syrup
1 cup apple cider or juice, divided
salt
4 firm red apples, unpeeled and thinly sliced
1 tablespoon vegetable oil
8 chicken thighs, skinned and boned
freshly ground black pepper
1 teaspoon dried thyme
1 cup shredded sharp cheddar

JULIE DeMATTEO, CLEMENTON, NEW JERSEY

"I love to take a recipe and play around. I had my mother's apple pie with cheddar cheese in mind, and the fact that I've always liked chicken and apples together."

GOING WILD

The town of Muscoda in the rolling hills of western Wisconsin was, for many years, host to the annual Morel Mushroom Festival, complete with rides, contests, and music. Hunters from the area, however, know you don't need a festival to celebrate the elusive morel. After a long day of tromping in the woods, enduring brambles and backache, squinting into the brush, and getting lost, you'll find that a meal of buttery, sautéed morels isn't just a special occasion, it's a triumph.

So it is with many edibles which are gathered and hunted around the state. Delicious, wholesome, and, best of all, *free*, wild foods are all around us. They rarely come easily but they're always worth the effort. Here are a few Wisconsin favorites:

- Spring: maple syrup, fiddlehead ferns, watercress, morel mushrooms, ramps, dandelions, honey, strawberries, and asparagus
- Summer: horseradish, crayfish, edible greens, raspberries, elderberries, blueberries, wild rice, mint, ginseng, and fish
- Fall and Winter: puffballs, wild grapes, acorns, hickory nuts, cranberries, deer, partridge, grouse, turkey, pheasant, duck, geese, and fish.

MIDWESTERN PORK CHOPS
WITH APPLE HORSERADISH SAUCE

Honorable Mention, 1998

Heat broiler. Place pork chops on foil-lined broiler pan. Melt 2 tablespoons apple jelly; brush chops with half the melted jelly. Broil 6 to 7 minutes. Turn and brush other side with remaining melted jelly. Broil until done, 6 to 9 minutes longer.

Meanwhile, heat butter in skillet over medium flame. Stir in apples; stir and cook 1 minute. Stir in remaining 2 tablespoons apple jelly and remaining ingredients (except fresh parsley). Cook, stirring often, until apples are barely tender, 3 to 5 minutes.

Arrange pork chops on serving platter. Spoon hot apple sauce over chops. Garnish with parsley sprigs.

Makes 4 servings.

4 pork loin chops,
  $3/4$-inch thick
4 tablespoons apple jelly,
  divided
2 tablespoons butter
2 medium tart apples,
  peeled and chopped
1 tablespoon cream-style
  horseradish
$1/2$ teaspoon dried
  rosemary
$1/2$ teaspoon dried parsley
salt and freshly ground
  black pepper to taste
fresh parsley sprigs for
  garnish

DIANE SPARROW, OSAGE, IOWA

ITALIAN SAUSAGE AND ROASTED GARLIC POTATO PIE

6 to 8 whole cloves fresh garlic

2 teaspoons olive oil

salt and freshly ground black pepper

1 ½ pounds bulk Italian sausage, hot or mild

1 cup chopped onion

1 tablespoon minced garlic

¾ cup frozen peas

1 cup half-and-half or heavy cream, divided

1 egg, lightly beaten

1 teaspoon ground cumin

5 dashes bottled hot pepper sauce

pinch paprika

2 ½ pounds Russet potatoes, peeled and cut

3 tablespoons butter

2 teaspoons chopped fresh rosemary

Remove outer papery skin, but do not peel, garlic cloves. Place whole cloves in clay garlic roaster or aluminum foil. Drizzle olive oil over garlic; sprinkle with salt and pepper. Cover clay roaster or fold foil around garlic securely. Place in oven; set temperature to 400 degrees, and bake until garlic is very tender, 45 to 50 minutes.

Meanwhile, heat large heavy skillet over medium-high flame. Add sausage and brown it, stirring to break it up as it cooks. Remove meat with a slotted spoon to bowl. Discard all but 1 tablespoon fat in skillet. Add onion and minced garlic; cook, stirring occasionally, until tender, 3 to 5 minutes. Transfer onion mixture to bowl with sausage. Stir in peas, ⅓ cup of the half-and-half, egg, cumin, pepper sauce, and paprika. Grease a glass or ceramic baking dish or casserole. Transfer sausage mixture to prepared dish.

Bring large pot of salted water to boil, add potatoes, and cook until tender, 15 to 20 minutes. Drain. Squeeze roasted garlic "meat" from skins; add to potatoes. Mash gently. Mix in butter, remaining ⅔ cup half-and-half, rosemary, and salt and pepper to taste. Spread over sausage.

Heat oven to 350 degrees. Bake pie 35 to 45 minutes.

Makes 6 to 8 servings.

Zita Wilensky, North Miami Beach, Florida

BRAISED PORK ROAST WITH RED WINE AND HERBS

Heat oven to 250 degrees. Place salt pork in Dutch oven or large, heavy pot. Cook over medium heat until browned. Remove with slotted spoon; set aside. Discard any fat in the pot. Add olive oil and heat it briefly over the flame. Add onions and garlic; cook, stirring often, until tender, 10 to 15 minutes. Remove and reserve with salt pork. Raise heat to medium high. Season pork butt with salt and pepper, add to pot, and brown on all sides.

Return salt pork and onion mixture to pot. Add tomatoes (with liquid), wine, bay leaf, orange zest, thyme, marjoram, and basil. Bring to simmer, cover pot tightly, and place in oven. Cook roast until meat is very tender, about 4 hours.

Remove meat to cutting board, cover, and let rest 10 minutes. Meanwhile, skim fat from sauce in pot and remove bay leaf. Bring to simmer over medium flame. Mix flour with 1 ½ tablespoons water and whisk into sauce until thickened. (Increase thickness by adding more flour-water mixture, if desired.) Slice meat and serve with thickened sauce. Garnish with fresh herbs.

Makes 10 or more servings.

2-inch-square piece of salt pork, minced

3 tablespoons olive oil

2 cups thinly sliced onions

4 teaspoons minced garlic

5-pound boneless Boston pork butt

salt and freshly ground black pepper

approximately 3 pounds fresh or canned plum tomatoes, coarsely chopped (reserve the liquid)

2 ½ cups hearty, dry red wine

1 bay leaf

1 tablespoon grated orange zest (grate only outermost, orange part of rind)

1 teaspoon each chopped fresh thyme and marjoram, or ½ teaspoon of each dried

4 tablespoons chopped fresh basil, or 1 ½ tablespoons dried

1 ½ tablespoons flour

chopped fresh herbs for garnish

MARILYN CLAY, PALATINE, ILLINOIS

"Toasted hazelnut mashed potatoes go well with this dish; use a drizzle of the sauce over them as well."

EASY CHINESE PORK

1 tablespoon dark sesame oil

1/3 cup dry sherry

1/4 cup soy sauce

1 tablespoon honey

1/4 teaspoon red pepper flakes (optional), or more to taste

1 pound pork tenderloin, cut into 1/2-inch rounds or 3/4-inch pieces

2 tablespoons brown sugar

1 tablespoon cornstarch

1/2 cup chicken stock or beer

cooked white or brown rice

2 tablespoons chopped green onion

Combine sesame oil, sherry, soy sauce, honey, and red pepper flakes (if desired) in medium bowl; mix well to dissolve honey. Add pork and marinate at room temperature 30 minutes or in refrigerator several hours.

Heat large skillet over medium-high flame. Add pork with marinade and bring to strong simmer. Whisk brown sugar, cornstarch, and stock or beer in small bowl; stir into simmering pork until thickened. Reduce heat to low, cover, and let mixture simmer until meat is cooked through, 6 to 8 minutes. Serve over rice and sprinkle with chopped green onions.

Makes 3 to 4 servings.

Daniel Yeh, Lodi, Wisconsin

BAKED PORK CHOPS AND BARLEY

Heat oven to 350 degrees. Heat olive oil in large, heavy skillet over medium-high heat. Add pork chops and brown well on both sides. Season with salt and pepper to taste, then remove to a platter. Reduce heat to medium, add onion to pan, and cook, stirring often, until they just begin to soften. Stir in beef or chicken broth, barley, and soy sauce, scraping up any bits stuck to bottom of skillet. Season with salt and pepper to taste (if you've used canned stock, take care not to over-salt the mixture). Pour barley mixture into a 9-by-13-inch baking dish. Arrange pork chops on top. Cover tightly with aluminum foil. Bake until pork chops and barley are tender and all the liquid has been absorbed, 50 to 60 minutes.

Makes 4 servings.

1 tablespoon olive oil

4 pork chops, at least 1-inch thick and trimmed of excess fat

salt and freshly ground black pepper

1 cup chopped onion

2 cups beef or chicken broth

$2/3$ cup medium pearled barley

1 tablespoon soy sauce

CHRISTINE KLESSIG, AMHERST JUNCTION, WISCONSIN

HONEY BARBECUED RIBS

4 pounds country-style pork ribs or pork spare ribs

2 teaspoons salt plus more to taste, divided

1 ½ cups ketchup

1 cup honey

½ cup finely chopped onion

2 tablespoons red wine or balsamic vinegar

2 tablespoons bottled steak sauce

2 teaspoons Dijon-style mustard

freshly ground black pepper to taste

Place pork ribs in large pot with 2 teaspoons salt and enough cold water to barely cover meat. Bring to slow simmer and cook over low heat ½ hour.

Meanwhile, mix ketchup, honey, onion, vinegar, steak sauce, and mustard in saucepan. Bring to simmer over low heat. Simmer 10 to 15 minutes. Season with remaining salt and pepper to taste.

Heat oven to 350 degrees. Drain ribs well. Place in shallow baking pans (for easy cleanup, pans may be lined first with aluminum foil or parchment paper). Pour sauce evenly over ribs. Bake until very tender, basting every 10 to 15 minutes with the sauce, 45 to 60 minutes.

Makes 8 to 10 servings.

JULIE RINDT, ANTIGO, WISCONSIN

"These ribs can also be put on an outdoor charcoal grill and basted with the sauce until done."

LAAB (LAOTIAN GROUND ROUND BEEF ROLL-UPS)

Place ground round in pot with enough cold water to barely cover. Bring to simmer and cook gently until medium-well done. Do not overcook. Drain and let cool. Place rice cereal in a heavy, preferably cast iron, skillet. Heat over medium flame, tossing occasionally, until grains are lightly browned. Let cool. Mix cooked beef, rice grains, green onions, spearmint, lime or lemon juice, ground chile, cilantro, and salt.

To serve, mound beef mixture on lettuce leaves on a large platter. Serve with sweet or long-grain rice and a vegetable tray that includes lettuce leaves and a variety of accompaniments from the list. Diners make "roll-ups" with the lettuce or cabbage leaves, meat, and accompaniments.

Serves 6 to 8 people.

3 pounds ground round beef

1/3 cup uncooked cream of rice cereal

1 cup thinly sliced green onions

1 cup finely chopped fresh spearmint leaves

juice of 4 limes or 2 lemons

2 teaspoons coarsely ground dried red chile or red pepper flakes

2 tablespoons chopped cilantro

2 teaspoons salt or to taste

lettuce leaves

cooked sweet rice or long-grain white rice

Accompaniments
lettuce leaves
green cabbage leaves
sliced green onions
sliced cucumber
chopped tomatoes
whole spearmint leaves
sliced raw green beans
sliced pickles
sliced olives

Wanchalee Pochanayon, Kenosha, Wisconsin

"I have a friend who calls these 'Thai tacos.' I learned how to make them from my mom. She'd look at a recipe, go to the store to buy the ingredients, then come home and make it her own way."

SOUTHERN SPOON BREAD SUPPER

1 pound ground round beef

1/2 cup finely chopped onions

1/2 cup finely chopped red bell pepper

1 cup shredded cheddar cheese, divided

freshly ground black pepper

1 cup stone-ground yellow cornmeal

2 teaspoons sugar

1 teaspoon salt

2 cups boiling water

1 cup milk

3 eggs

3 tablespoons melted butter

1 teaspoon baking powder

Heat oven to 400 degrees. Grease a 2- or 2 ½-quart non-metal baking dish. Heat a medium-size skillet over medium-high heat. Add ground round and brown it, breaking it up occasionally, until nearly done. Add onions and red bell pepper. Cook, stirring often, until ground round is completely done and vegetables are limp. Stir in ½ cup of the cheddar and pepper to taste. Set aside.

Combine cornmeal, sugar, salt, and boiling water in a saucepan. Place over low heat and cook, stirring often, until mixture is thick and smooth. Remove from heat and slowly add milk, stirring constantly. Beat in eggs, one at a time. Stir in melted butter and baking powder; beat until batter is well blended. Stir in meat mixture. Spread mixture in prepared dish. Sprinkle remaining ½ cup of cheese over surface of mixture. Bake until spoon bread is firm in middle, 30 to 45 minutes.

Makes 6 servings.

ROSEMARY JOHNSON, BIRMINGHAM, ALABAMA

OLD-FASHIONED BEEF, BACON, AND SAUERKRAUT CASSEROLE

Heat oven to 350 degrees. Grease a medium baking dish. Dice bacon and fry over medium heat until medium-crisp. Drain bacon on paper towel; discard all but 3 tablespoons of bacon grease in the pan. Add hamburger and onions to the pan and cook until hamburger is browned and onions are limp. Stir in rice and sauerkraut (if you prefer a looser mixture, add ½ cup water, also); mix well and place in baking dish. Mix tomato soup and sugar in small bowl; pour over top of casserole. Sprinkle bacon bits over tomato mixture. Bake 1 hour.

Makes 4 servings.

4 to 5 strips bacon (Hillshire Farms is recommended)

1 ½ pounds hamburger

1 cup chopped onion

1 cup instant long-grain rice

1 can (14 ounces) sauerkraut (Frank's, a Wisconsin brand, is recommended), drained

1 can (10 ¾ ounces) tomato soup

4 teaspoons brown sugar

CHARLOTTE MATCHA, WAUKESHA, WISCONSIN

BROCCOLI BEEF PIE

1 pound ground beef
1/4 cup chopped onion
1 teaspoon minced garlic
2 tablespoons flour
3/4 teaspoon salt
freshly ground black pepper
1 1/4 cups milk
1 small package (3 ounces) cream cheese, softened
1 egg, beaten
2 cups chopped, blanched fresh broccoli or 1 package (10 ounces) frozen, chopped broccoli, thawed and drained well
pastry dough for double-crust pie
4 ounces sliced Monterey Jack or mozzarella cheese
additional milk

Heat oven to 350 degrees. Heat skillet over medium flame. Add ground beef, onions, and garlic and cook, stirring often, until beef is browned and onions are limp. Lower heat, stir in flour, salt and pepper to taste, and cook briefly, stirring constantly. Mix in milk and softened cream cheese. Continue to stir and cook until mixture is smooth and bubbly. Remove about 1 cup of the mixture from the skillet and stir it into the beaten egg, then stir egg mixture into skillet. Cook and stir until mixture is thick. Fold in broccoli. Turn off the heat.

Roll out pastry dough into two pie rounds. Line a pie pan with one of the rounds. Spoon beef mixture into pie pan and arrange cheese slices over mixture. Top with second pie round; trim and crimp edges to seal pie. Make a few slits in top of pie to allow steam to escape. Brush top crust with a little milk. Bake 40 to 45 minutes. Let stand 10 minutes before serving.

Makes 6 servings.

KATHRYN GREFE, MAUSTON, WISCONSIN

PICANTE PORK BARBECUE SANDWICHES

Heat oil in medium saucepan over medium-high flame. Add meat chunks and brown on all sides. Add picante sauce, brown sugar, Worcestershire sauce, chili powder, and ½ cup water. Stir well and bring to a boil. Reduce heat to low, cover pan, and slowly simmer the meat, stirring occasionally, 30 minutes. Remove pork from pan and keep warm. Raise heat under sauce and simmer vigorously, uncovered, until sauce is thickened, 5 to 10 minutes. Season sauce with salt to taste. Slice or chop pork loin and return it to the pan to coat it with sauce. You can serve it right away or let it cool and chill to develop flavor. Reheat briefly just before serving.

To serve, spoon equal amounts of meat onto bottoms of four sandwich buns. Top with equal portions of coleslaw and tops of buns. Serve immediately.

Makes 4 servings.

1 tablespoon vegetable oil

1 pound boneless pork loin, cut into 4 large chunks

1 jar (16 ounces) mild or medium-hot picante sauce

2 tablespoons packed brown sugar

2 tablespoons Worcestershire sauce

1 teaspoon chili powder

salt

4 sandwich buns, split

1 cup coleslaw

LISA KEYS, MIDDLEBURY, CONNECTICUT

FLORENTINE STUFFED SHELLS

1 package (10 ounces) frozen chopped spinach, thawed, or 1 pound blanched fresh spinach, chopped*

1 container (15 ounces) light ricotta cheese

½ cup freshly grated parmesan cheese

1 egg, beaten

1 teaspoon Curt's Premium Blend Cooking Spice (or other bottled seasoning spice)

1 tablespoon each chopped fresh oregano and basil, or 1 teaspoon of each dried

1 can (28 ounces) Italian-style chopped tomatoes

20 jumbo pasta shells, cooked "firm"

½ cup shredded low-fat mozzarella cheese

*For instructions, see page 44.

Heat oven to 350 degrees. Drain spinach well and combine with ricotta, parmesan, egg, cooking spice, oregano, and basil. Spread two-thirds of the chopped tomatoes on bottom of 8-by-8-inch baking dish. Fill shells with spinach-cheese mixture; arrange over tomatoes. Pour remaining tomatoes over shells. Cover and bake 20 minutes. Uncover, sprinkle on the mozzarella, and bake 10 to 15 minutes longer. The shells can also be cooked in a covered aluminum foil pan on a grill.

Makes 6 to 8 servings.

NANCY F. RAFAL, BAILEYS HARBOR, WISCONSIN

"This makes a good picnic side dish because it stays hot for a long time and is easy to 'serve yourself.' The recipe is easily doubled for an 11-by-14-inch pan."

BEEF, MUSHROOM, AND BLACK OLIVE OVEN STEW

··

The flavor of this stew improves as it "ages," so make it in the morning or a day ahead, if possible. Heat oven to 325 degrees. Heat 1 tablespoon olive oil in large, heavy Dutch oven over medium-high heat. Brown beef cubes in batches, without crowding the pan. As each batch is browned, salt and pepper it lightly and transfer to a bowl. Use a bit more olive oil with each batch as needed. After all the beef is browned, reduce the heat to medium-low, add the onions to the pot, and cook, stirring often, until nearly tender. Add the garlic and continue to cook a couple of minutes longer. Return beef to pot. Whisk the flour into the beef stock and add this mixture to the pot along with the tomato sauce, parsley, basil or oregano, and bay leaf. Bring to simmer, cover tightly, and place in oven.

Let stew simmer gently in oven (check it after about 15 minutes and lower oven heat to 300 if stew is simmering hard or is boiling) until beef is tender, 1 to 2 hours. Remove bay leaf. Stir in mushrooms and olives. Cover and continue to cook in oven until mushrooms are tender, 20 to 30 minutes. Because of the olives, you probably won't need additional salt in this stew, but do add pepper to taste. Serve over wide egg noodles, pasta, rice, or dumplings.

Makes 6 servings.

2 or more tablespoons olive oil, divided

2 1/2 to 3 pounds beef stew meat or chuck roast, cut into 1-inch cubes

salt and freshly ground black pepper

2 medium onions, thinly sliced

2 to 3 teaspoons minced garlic

2 tablespoons flour

2 cups homemade beef stock or 1 can (14 1/2 ounces) beef broth

1 can (8 ounces) tomato sauce

1 tablespoon dried parsley

1 teaspoon dried basil or oregano

1 bay leaf

2 cups quartered fresh mushrooms (white, shiitake, or brown)*

3/4 cup Greek olives, pitted and coarsely chopped

*Or use a mixture of fresh and dried mushrooms, e.g., 1 cup fresh shiitake, 1/4 cup dried porcini, 3/4 cup dried morels.

··

CHRISTINE KLESSIG, AMHERST JUNCTION, WISCONSIN

SAVORY HAM AND POTATO BAKE

2 tablespoons butter

2 tablespoons flour

1 teaspoon dry mustard, or 1 tablespoon prepared Dijon-style mustard

2/3 cup milk, warm or at room temperature

1 1/2 cups (about 6 ounces) shredded mild cheddar (or other cheese), divided

4 cups peeled and cubed potatoes, cooked

1 1/2 cups chopped ham

1/4 cup chopped green onions

salt and freshly ground black pepper

Heat oven to 350 degrees. Grease a 1 1/2- to 2-quart casserole dish. Melt butter in saucepan over low heat. Whisk in flour until smooth. Cook, stirring often, 2 to 3 minutes. Stir in mustard. Gradually whisk in milk, then stir constantly until mixture thickens. Stir in 1 cup of the grated cheese until completely melted. Remove from heat. Fold in potatoes, ham, green onions, and salt and pepper to taste. Bake 30 minutes. Sprinkle remaining 1/2 cup cheese over top of casserole and continue to bake until cheese is melted. Let stand 5 minutes before serving.

Makes 4 to 6 servings.

Patricia Janke, Iola, Wisconsin

STUFFED PORK LOIN ROAST WITH RASPBERRY SAUCE

Melt butter in skillet over medium heat. Add onion and celery. Cook, stirring often, 2 to 3 minutes. Stir in apples and continue cooking until vegetables are tender. Grind the dried bread cubes in food processor or blender. Combine onion mixture with bread crumbs, raisins, and allspice in a bowl. Season with salt and pepper to taste. Cool mixture completely.

Heat oven to 325 degrees. Slit the roast nearly in half lengthwise so it opens like a long book. Spoon stuffing over half of the roast and close the "book." Tie the roast with cooking string or secure it with toothpicks at the edge. Place in lightly oiled roasting pan that's just large enough to hold it (fat side up). Roast until pork is done, about 1 hour.

Meanwhile, make a sauce: combine raspberries, jam, and brandy in small saucepan. Bring to strong simmer, stirring. Remove from heat and strain out the seeds through a fine-mesh sieve. Keep warm. When pork is done, let roast stand 5 to 10 minutes before slicing. Serve with raspberry sauce.

Makes 6 servings.

1/4 cup butter or margarine
1/2 cup finely chopped onion
1/4 cup finely chopped celery
1 medium tart apple, peeled and chopped
2 cups dried-out bread cubes (if you have only fresh bread, dry it out in a hot oven first)
1/4 cup raisins
1/4 teaspoon allspice
salt and freshly ground black pepper
2 pounds boneless pork loin roast
1 cup drained raspberries, fresh or thawed
1/4 cup seedless raspberry jam
1 tablespoon brandy

ANNE MEANS, MADISON, WISCONSIN

GARLIC CHICKEN "WHITE" PIZZA

dough for 12-inch pizza crust

cornmeal

½ cup sour cream

½ cup mayonnaise

3 tablespoons freshly grated parmesan cheese

2 to 3 teaspoons minced garlic

2 tablespoons chopped fresh oregano or basil, or 2 teaspoons dried

½ cup finely chopped onion

1 ½ cups chopped cooked chicken

1 to 2 cups sliced mushrooms

optional: chopped sweet or hot peppers, zucchini, or green olives

1 to 2 cups shredded mozzarella cheese

Heat oven to 400 degrees (if you are using a baking stone, heat it in the oven at least ½ hour). Sprinkle a pizza "paddle" or heavy baking sheet with cornmeal. Roll or pat pizza dough into a 12-inch circle. Transfer to baking stone with the paddle or place it on the baking sheet. Bake crust 4 to 5 minutes.

Make a sauce by combining the sour cream, mayonnaise, parmesan, garlic, and herbs. Spread sauce evenly over partially cooked crust. Distribute remaining ingredients as desired over sauce. Bake 12 to 15 minutes longer.

Makes 4 servings.

Colleen L. Rosga, Oregon, Wisconsin

SHARON'S PORK ROAST WITH GARLIC MUSTARD SAUCE

···

Allow pork roast to come to room temperature, about 1 hour. Heat oven to 350 degrees. Mix garlic, mustard, soy sauce, olive oil, parsley, ginger, and pepper in small bowl. Brush half of the mixture over entire roast. Place meat fat side up on rack in roasting pan. Bake until internal temperature taken with an instant thermometer reads 155 to 160 degrees, about 1 ½ to 2 hours (internal temperature will continue to rise about 5 more degrees after roast is removed from oven). Remove from oven and let stand 10 minutes before slicing. Meanwhile, gently heat remaining sauce. Cut roast into fairly thick slices and serve with warm mustard sauce.

Makes 12 or more servings.

4 to 5 pound boneless rolled pork roast

2 teaspoons minced garlic, mashed to a paste with fork or flat of knife

½ cup Dijon-style mustard

2 tablespoons soy sauce

2 tablespoons olive oil

2 tablespoons dried parsley flakes

2 teaspoons minced fresh ginger, mashed to a paste, or ½ teaspoon ground ginger

½ teaspoon cracked black pepper

···

SHARON BURDICK, RACINE, WISCONSIN

"This is delicious with asparagus spears and boiled red potatoes that have been tossed with melted butter, chopped green onions, and fresh parsley."

BEER: IT'S WHAT'S FOR DINNER

Brown ales, pale ales, stouts, bocks, pilsners, porters, Belgians, bitters. They're pouring out of regional microbreweries, local brewpubs, and homebrew kitchens. They're featured at beer tastings and brew festivals.

Beer has been a hit in Wisconsin ever since European immigrants first realized that the area's clear waters and cold temperatures were made to order for brewing. In the 20th century, we weathered the decades when streamlined, corporate beers eclipsed the artisanal choices made by the little guys. And these days, if ever there was a "food" trend made to order for the state, it's the current lust for unique, local brews.

Beer connoisseurs love to pair their favorites with two other state specialties, cheese and sausage. Like wine experts, they can also match beer in all its forms and flavors with a spectrum of foodstuffs and recipes. At home, folks are even cooking with beer.

If you're new at using beer as a recipe ingredient, here are a few tips to keep in mind:

- Use beer's natural bitterness to harmonize with the sweetness of such cooked vegetables as onions, carrots, and corn.
- Substitute beer for other liquids like wine, stock, and water in soups and sauces but keep in mind that its flavor intensifies with long simmering.
- Beer-based marinades give lots of flavor without the acidity of vinegar or lemon juice.
- Beer added to batters makes pancakes and fritters more tender and tasty.
- Remember that if a particular beer would taste good *with* a particular dish, it would probably also be delicious *in* that dish.

BEEF AND BEER STEW
WITH HERB DUMPLINGS

Film the bottom of a large heavy skillet with olive oil and heat over medium-high flame. Dredge beef cubes in seasoned flour. Shake off excess flour and brown the beef in batches (do not crowd the pan), adding a bit more oil with each batch as needed. Transfer browned beef to a Dutch oven as each batch is done. When all the beef is browned, stir the beef broth into the pan and bring it to a boil, scraping up any bits in the pan. Add the hot broth to the beef, along with the beer, garlic, parsley, and bay leaf. Bring to simmer, lower heat, and cook very gently until beef is barely tender, about 1 hour or longer.

Add all the vegetables and season stew with salt and pepper. Return to simmer, cover, and cook gently until vegetables are tender, about 30 minutes. Flavor is best if you cool the stew and chill it several hours or overnight.

Reheat the stew to simmering. To make dumpling batter, combine flour, baking powder, salt, and herbs in medium bowl. Beat egg and milk in small bowl. Stir milk mixture into flour mixture until just combined. Drop spoonfuls of batter on surface of stew, leaving some space between each dumpling. Cover tightly and simmer gently about 12 minutes, until toothpick inserted in center of dumpling comes out clean. Serve immediately.

Makes 6 to 8 servings.

Adapted from a recipe by Patricia S. Orcutt, Wisconsin Rapids, Wisconsin

Stew
olive oil

2 pounds cubed beef chuck

flour seasoned with salt and pepper

1 1/2 cups beef broth

1 bottle (12 ounces) dark beer

2 teaspoons minced garlic

2 teaspoons dried parsley

1 bay leaf

1 large onion, cut into chunks

4 stalks celery, cut into small chunks

4 medium carrots, cut into small chunks

2 medium potatoes, scrubbed and cut into chunks

1 large tomato, cut into chunks

salt and freshly ground black pepper to taste

Dumplings
1 3/4 cups flour

3 teaspoons baking powder

1/2 teaspoon salt

2 teaspoons each chopped fresh parsley, sage, and chives, or 1/2 teaspoon of each dried

1 teaspoon chopped fresh rosemary, or 1/4 teaspoon dried

1 egg

2/3 cup milk

4

BAKED GOODS and BREAKFAST/BRUNCH ITEMS

A satellite photo of Wisconsin taken at night offers a telling picture of the state's population spread. The night view highlights splashes of bright light that indicate towns and cities; between them are dark stretches, evidence of forests and farmlands. Even in the southeastern portion of the state, where a glowing queue of urban centers outlines the Lake Michigan shoreline, shaded regions lie not far away. No matter where you look on the speckled map, the city remains close to the country.

So it is with Wisconsinites and the foods we eat. Most of us reside in or near a metropolitan area and live a typically modern life. We are, however, surrounded by our rural roots; and our agricultural heritage, past and present, shows on our menus.

Granted, most home cooks no longer milk cows or pluck chicken feathers. Few make cheese at home or stuff chopped meat into sausage casings. Even the number of people who process fruit preserves or can pickles is diminishing. But one farm-based practice we haven't given up on altogether is baking. There is slow-paced, country-style joy in mixing biscuit dough or watching a pan of buttermilk rolls rise. The basic ingredients of home baking—eggs, flour, milk— are farmhouse staples, while the goodies we add to many pastries—fruits, nuts, honey—come from field and orchard.

Country Mornings

Homemade breads and pastries are consumed throughout the day, but we associate them first with the morning meal. The sweet aroma of baked goods hot from the oven, like the blueberry cream-cheese coffee cake or the puffy raspberry pancake from this section, signals homespun goodness. Busy diners who survive on take-out food and TV dinners from Monday through Friday find a kind of weekend retreat in baking a batch of cranberry muffins on a lazy Saturday morning. We may not have time to bake yeast breads every day, but we can manage a loaf of quick bread for a Sunday breakfast, and while it's browning in the oven, there's time to work on the rest of the meal.

The days of hard, physical labor and big farm breakfasts may be disappearing, but it's still possible to enjoy an old-fashioned gathering around the table at a weekend brunch. It's not a daily ritual, it's an occasion. So we go all out, flipping omelettes and frying bacon, brewing coffee from fresh-ground whole beans. Or we make something different, something special, something, perhaps, from the pages that follow: a frittata with chopped broccoli, a stack of potato pancakes topped with applesauce, a fruit-filled clafouti. When we make it ourselves, the whole meal is enhanced, whether we share it with others or spend the morning alone with the *New York Times*.

While restaurants entice us with brunch buffets and local bakeries supply everything from crullers to croissants, they can't bestow the folksy pleasures that come from making something from scratch, in our own kitchen, on our own terms. Like some of the cooks in this chapter, we may weave newer styles and unusual ingredients into our morning fare—a cheese-topped apple "pizza" or a southwestern-style breakfast strata, for example—but no matter what and when we choose to bake, we are yielding to the nostalgic tug of country living.

Staying Grounded

Besides encouraging us to bake and to enjoy "slow" foods, our rural heritage colors how we acquire ingredients and where we dine out, reconnecting us to the land in numerous ways. Deer hunting and morel gathering are annual traditions in many families. Backyard gardens yield homegrown produce and earthy satisfactions. During the warm months, farmers' markets and roadside stands spring up around the region, drawing shoppers eager for a taste of honest food.

Communities mark the season with crop and harvest festivals, celebrating cranberries, strawberries, sweet corn, apples, maple syrup, and more. Families attend church suppers and community picnics, and travelers seek out small-town cafes, just for the simple, country fun of it. Like baking from scratch, these experiences slow us down, bring us together, and remind us of a time when life was less complicated.

BROCCOLI AND PASTA FRITTATA

Break angel-hair pasta strands in half. Boil pasta in salted water until tender; drain well and let cool several minutes. Meanwhile, steam broccoli until crisp-tender, about 2 minutes. Rinse with cool water and drain well. Mix pasta, broccoli, green onions, and olive oil in large bowl. Stir in cheeses, eggs, chopped fresh herbs (if desired), and pepper to taste. Mix well.

Heat 1 tablespoon butter in large nonstick skillet over medium-high flame. Spread pasta mixture evenly in skillet. Reduce heat to medium and cook frittata until mostly set and lightly colored on the bottom, 8 to 10 minutes. Loosen around edges of, and underneath, frittata with a spatula. Wearing oven mitts on both hands, place a large plate over skillet and invert frittata onto the plate. Heat remaining 1 tablespoon butter in skillet. Slide frittata back into the skillet and continue to cook until completely set and lightly colored on the bottom. Loosen sides and bottom of frittata, slide onto plate, and cut into wedges to serve. This is delicious with a cooked tomato sauce or salsa.

Makes 4 to 6 servings.

1/4 pound angel-hair pasta

1 1/2 cups broccoli florets, cut into 1/2-inch pieces

1/4 cup chopped green onions

2 tablespoons olive oil

1/2 cup shredded provolone or mozzarella cheese

1/4 cup freshly grated parmesan cheese

2 eggs, beaten

2 to 3 tablespoons chopped fresh dill or basil (optional)

freshly grated black pepper

2 tablespoons butter, divided

ANNE MEANS, MADISON, WISCONSIN

SAGEBRUSH STRATA

Winner, 1998

1 can (15 ounces) black beans, rinsed and drained

½ cup cooked corn kernels

¼ cup minced green onion

4 eggs

1 ½ cups milk

1 cup tomato salsa

½ cup sour cream

½ teaspoon cumin

5 six-inch flour tortillas

½ cup shredded sharp cheddar cheese

cilantro or parsley sprigs for garnish

Combine beans, corn, and green onions in bowl. Whisk eggs and milk in second bowl. Combine salsa, sour cream, and cumin in third bowl. Oil a 6-cup soufflé dish or baking dish. To make strata, place a tortilla in bottom of baking dish. Spread a quarter of the bean mixture on tortilla. Pour on a quarter of the milk mixture. Repeat layers three more times, ending with a tortilla. Spread sour cream mixture over top tortilla. Cover and refrigerate overnight.

Heat oven to 350 degrees. Sprinkle cheese over strata. Bring about 2 quarts of water to boiling. Place strata dish in large pan; pour enough boiling water into pan to reach halfway up baking dish. Bake until firm, about 1 hour. Serve hot or at room temperature. Garnish with cilantro or parsley.

Makes 4 to 6 servings.

Roxanne E. Chan, Albany, California

"I'm big on dairy products because they're the 'real thing.'"

SWEET AND WHITE POTATO BURRITOS

Winner, 1998

Cook potatoes in boiling water until nearly tender, about 10 minutes. Drain, reserving ⅓ cup cooking liquid.

Heat peanut oil in large skillet over medium heat; add onions and sauté until tender, about 5 minutes. Add potatoes, cilantro, chili powder, oregano, cayenne, reserved liquid, and salt and pepper to taste; toss gently. Raise heat to medium-high and cook mixture, stirring occasionally, until potatoes are tender, about 5 minutes.

Spoon a cup or more of potatoes down center of each tortilla. Fold sides in over filling and roll up. Serve with guacamole or salsa.

Makes 8 servings.

3 large sweet potatoes, peeled and cut into 1-inch chunks

3 medium white potatoes, peeled and cut into 1-inch chunks

2 tablespoons peanut oil

1 large sweet onion, chopped

¼ cup chopped cilantro

3 teaspoons chili powder

1 teaspoon dried oregano

¼ teaspoon or more cayenne pepper

salt and freshly ground black pepper

8 ten-inch flour tortillas (plain, spinach-, or sun-dried-tomato-flavored), warmed

spicy guacamole or fruit salsa

DIANE HALFERTY, TUCSON, ARIZONA

NEW POTATO PANCAKES

2 eggs
1 medium onion
1 pound red potatoes
6 to 8 tablespoons
    cracker crumbs
$1/2$ teaspoon salt
$1/2$ teaspoon ground
    black pepper
butter
vegetable oil

Accompaniments
(*choose one or more
    of the following*)
cooked bacon bits
applesauce
sour cream and chives
cottage cheese blended
    with fresh herbs
cranberry sauce
maple syrup

Beat eggs in large bowl. Grate the onion into the eggs. Peel (or partially peel) the potatoes and grate them on large holes of hand-held grater. Squeeze grated potatoes to remove some of the excess liquid. You should have about 2 heaping cups. Stir potatoes into egg mixture. Stir in cracker crumbs (use the larger amount if mixture is loose), salt, and pepper. Heat heavy or cast iron pan over medium heat. For each batch of pancakes, heat enough butter and oil to film the bottom of the pan. Butter–oil mixture should be very hot before you add the batter. Scoop the batter into the pan ($1/4$ cup per pancake), pressing down to flatten each pancake. Fry until browned on both sides and tender in the middle. As you finish each batch, transfer the pancakes to a baking pan and keep them warm in the oven (or serve them straight from the skillet).

Makes about 8 four-inch pancakes.

ERIN SKORUPA, FOND DU LAC, WISCONSIN

CHEESE-KISSED APPLE TORTE "PIZZA"

Heat oven to 400 degrees. Roll out the pie dough to fit a 12-inch pizza pan and extend over the edge. Fold in and crimp the overlapping dough to create a neat edge.

Beat the egg, half-and-half, sugar, cinnamon, and nutmeg in a medium bowl. Peel the apples and cut each one into 12 slices. Arrange the apple slices on the crust in two or three concentric circles. Stir the egg mixture once again and gently pour it over apples. Bake torte 15 minutes, reduce the heat to 350 degrees, and continue baking until apples are tender and custard is set, 30 to 40 minutes. Remove from oven and sprinkle with cheddar. Return to oven and bake until cheese is melted, a few more minutes. Serve warm or at room temperature.

Makes 10 servings.

double recipe of pie crust dough
1 egg
1 cup half-and-half
1 cup sugar
$1/4$ teaspoon cinnamon
$1/4$ teaspoon nutmeg
5 large tart apples
1 to 2 cups shredded aged white cheddar cheese (or use a younger, yellow cheddar if desired)

MARGARET ZICKERT, DEERFIELD, WISCONSIN

"Our retirement income is a two-acre orchard so we have apples served in every way."

CHEESY GARLIC ROLLS

up to 5 ½ cups flour, divided

3 tablespoons sugar

2 teaspoons salt

1 package (¼ ounce) active dry yeast

1 ½ cups milk

½ cup (1 stick) butter, melted (divided)

2 tablespoons olive oil

2 teaspoons minced garlic

2 teaspoons dried chives

1 teaspoon dried Italian herb seasoning

⅔ cup grated sharp cheddar

Combine 3 cups flour, sugar, salt, and yeast in large bowl. Combine milk and ½ cup water in saucepan; heat to 120 degrees (an instant thermometer works well). Gradually stir milk mixture into flour mixture. Stir in ¼ cup melted butter. Beat at low speed with electric beaters about 30 seconds, then beat at high for 1 minute. Gradually stir in enough of the remaining flour to make a soft dough.

Turn dough onto floured surface; knead until smooth, 6 to 8 minutes. Place dough in large bowl, cover, and let rise in warm place until double in bulk, about 1 hour.

Punch down dough; cover and let rest 10 minutes. Combine remaining ¼ cup butter, olive oil, garlic, chives, and Italian seasoning in bowl.

Divide dough into 24 pieces. Place a heaping teaspoon of grated cheddar in center of each dough piece and roll it into a ball. Dip balls in butter mixture and place in muffin tin. Drizzle remaining butter mixture over dough balls. Cover and let rise in warm place until double in bulk, about 45 minutes. Meanwhile, heat oven to 375 degrees. Bake rolls until golden brown, 14 to 16 minutes. Serve warm.

Makes 24 rolls.

Roz Keimig, Guymon, Oklahoma

RISE AND DINE

We call it "breakfast" but maybe a more accurate term these days would be "fast break," for that is about all most folks have time to make in the morning. On special occasions, we might manage a leisurely brunch of omelettes, fresh-squeezed orange juice, and homemade coffee cake, but on workdays it's a packaged granola bar and out the door.

What today's schedule-impaired cook really wants is something in between: something tasty but healthful, something unique but easy to do. Here are some ideas for morning "fast foods" that hit all the right notes:

- Cinnamon apple toast: sauté sliced apples with maple syrup and mound on cinnamon toast
- Smoothies: low-fat yogurt blended with orange juice, banana, honey, and strawberries (or any fruit of choice)
- English muffin pizza: Italian tomato pasta sauce, chopped zucchini, and parmesan cheese broiled on English muffin halves
- Quesadilla: cheddar or feta cheese, green onions, and chopped cilantro layered between two corn tortillas and grilled
- Breakfast sundae: cantaloupe filled with cottage cheese and drizzled with puréed, sieved raspberries
- Smoked whitefish bagel: cream cheese, sliced tomatoes, and smoked fish on an onion bagel
- Maple fruit oatmeal: quick oats cooked with craisins or dried cherries, topped with maple syrup and nuts
- Chicken or vegetable hash: leftover potatoes, onions, and chicken or green vegetable topped with a purée of cottage cheese and fresh herbs.

ORANGE CRANBERRY HICKORY NUT MUFFINS

1 cup rolled oats (not instant)
1 cup orange juice
3 cups flour
1 cup sugar
1 teaspoon baking powder
½ teaspoon baking soda
1 cup vegetable oil
3 eggs, beaten
1 tablespoon grated orange zest (grate only outermost, orange-colored part of the rind)
1 ½ cups fresh or frozen cranberries (if using frozen cranberries, keep them frozen until ready to use)
½ cup chopped hickory nuts

Heat oven to 400 degrees. Grease muffin tins or line them with paper liners. Combine oats and orange juice in medium bowl; set aside briefly. In larger bowl, combine flour, sugar, baking powder, and baking soda. Stir oil, eggs, and orange zest into oat mixture. Stir wet mixture into flour mixture until barely combined. Fold in cranberries. Spoon batter into muffin cups, filling three-fourths full. Sprinkle hickory nuts over tops. Bake until toothpick inserted near center comes out clean, 13 to 15 minutes. Cool 10 minutes; remove muffins from tins. Serve warm.

Makes 16 to 20 muffins.

Genny Derer, Madison, Wisconsin

BLUEBERRY CREAM CHEESE COFFEE CAKE

Heat oven to 350 degrees. Grease a 9-by-13-inch baking pan or a 10-inch springform pan.

Cream butter, cream cheese, and sugar in large bowl. Stir in eggs, milk, 1 teaspoon vanilla, and cinnamon. Combine sifted flour, baking powder, and baking soda in separate bowl, then stir into butter mixture until barely combined. Gently fold in blueberries. Spread batter into prepared pan.

Make topping by combining brown sugar, flour, and cinnamon in a bowl. Cut in butter pieces with pastry blender or fingertips until mixture is crumbly. Sprinkle evenly over top of batter in pan. Bake until toothpick inserted near center comes out clean, 30 to 40 minutes. Cool.

Make glaze by mixing powdered sugar, milk, and ½ teaspoon vanilla. Drizzle glaze over cooled cake.

Makes 12 servings.

½ cup (1 stick) butter, softened
1 package (8 ounces) cream cheese, softened
1 cup sugar
2 eggs, beaten
⅓ cup milk
1 teaspoon vanilla extract
½ teaspoon cinnamon
2 cups sifted flour (sift before measuring)
1 teaspoon baking powder
½ teaspoon baking soda
1 heaping cup fresh or frozen blueberries (if using frozen berries, keep them frozen until ready to use)

Topping
½ cup brown sugar
½ cup flour
1 teaspoon cinnamon
3 tablespoons butter, cut into pieces

Glaze
1 cup powdered sugar
3 to 4 tablespoons milk
½ teaspoon vanilla extract

PATRICIA A. GELBUDA, TWO RIVERS, WISCONSIN

"Fresh raspberries can also be used [in place of the blueberries]. This keeps well and is absolutely delicious."

DOOR COUNTY CHERRY COFFEE CAKE

4 eggs

1 cup sugar, divided

½ cup (1 stick) butter, softened

1 teaspoon vanilla extract

1 cup sifted flour (sift before measuring)

2 cups tart cherries, fresh or frozen (if using frozen, keep them frozen until ready to use)

⅓ cup plus 1 tablespoon powdered sugar

Heat oven to 350 degrees. Grease an 8-by-8-inch baking pan or a 9 ½-inch pie tin.

Separate eggs, placing the whites in a clean, dry bowl and reserving the yolks. Beat egg whites at medium speed with electric beaters until foamy, 2 to 3 minutes. Raise speed to high, and continue to beat while you gradually add ¼ cup of the sugar. Continue beating until whites are stiff. Set aside.

Cream butter and remaining ¾ cup of sugar in large bowl. Stir in egg yolks, vanilla, and sifted flour. Stir in ¼ of the egg whites until well mixed. Gently fold in remaining egg whites with a spatula (a few "lumps" of egg white may remain). Spread batter into prepared pan. Distribute cherries over surface, then press them into the batter. Bake until toothpick inserted near center comes out clean, 30 to 40 minutes. Sift powdered sugar evenly over top of coffee cake while it is still hot (the powdered sugar will form a fairly heavy layer on top, but some will "melt" into the surface). Serve warm or at room temperature.

Makes 10 servings.

Margaret Zickert, Deerfield, Wisconsin

DRIED CRANBERRY FRUIT QUICK BREAD

Cream butter and honey in large bowl until well combined. Beat in eggs. Stir in mashed banana and cranberry juice. In a separate bowl, combine flour, cinnamon, baking powder, baking soda, and salt. Stir dry mixture into wet mixture until barely combined. Fold in apricots, dried cranberries, and nuts, taking care not to overmix. Oil one large or two small loaf pans. Spoon batter into prepared pan(s) and let stand 15 minutes while you heat the oven to 350 degrees. Bake bread until toothpick inserted near center comes out clean, 60 to 70 minutes for large pan, 50 to 60 minutes for small pans. Cool 5 minutes in pan(s) then remove bread to cool on wire rack.

Makes 1 large or 2 small loaves.

6 tablespoons butter or margarine, softened
$2/3$ cup honey
2 eggs
1 cup mashed ripe banana
3 tablespoons cranberry juice
2 cups flour
1 teaspoon cinnamon
1 teaspoon baking powder
$1/2$ teaspoon baking soda
$1/4$ teaspoon salt
$3/4$ cup diced dried apricots
1 cup dried cranberries
$1/4$ cup chopped walnuts or hickory nuts

SHIRLEY JOHNSON, WARRENS, WISCONSIN

APPLE RASPBERRY PANCAKES WITH RASPBERRY SAUCE

● ●

Sauce

1 cup raspberries (fresh, or frozen and thawed)

1 tablespoon sugar

1 to 2 tablespoons frozen apple juice concentrate

1/2 teaspoon grated lemon zest (grate only outermost, yellow part of rind)

Pancakes

2/3 cup apple juice

1/3 cup applesauce

1/4 teaspoon vanilla extract

1 tablespoon vegetable oil

1 egg, lightly beaten

1 cup flour

2 teaspoons baking powder

1/4 teaspoon cinnamon

3 tablespoons sugar

1/2 cup chopped, peeled apple

1/2 cup raspberries (fresh; or frozen, thawed, and drained)

Other ingredients

1/3 cup seedless raspberry jam, warmed (optional)

To make sauce: Combine all the sauce ingredients in a saucepan; mix well. Bring to strong simmer, stirring occasionally. Remove sauce from heat and strain through a fine mesh strainer to remove seeds. Keep sauce warm while you make the pancakes.

To make pancakes: Mix apple juice, applesauce, vanilla, oil, and egg in large bowl. Mix flour, baking powder, cinnamon, and sugar in a second bowl. Stir wet mixture into dry mixture until barely combined. Gently stir in chopped apples and raspberries. Heat a greased, heavy skillet or pancake griddle over medium flame. Scoop batter, 1/4 cup at a time, onto hot griddle. Cook until pancakes are golden on bottom, 2 to 3 minutes, then flip pancakes and cook until done, 2 to 3 minutes longer. Layer three pancakes onto individual plates, spreading warmed raspberry jam between the layers, if desired. Spoon the raspberry sauce over each stack and serve immediately.

Makes about 12 pancakes, or 4 pancake stacks.

● ●

MARIA THOMPSON, FRANKLIN, WISCONSIN

CHOICE FOODS

You see them in all but the smallest of towns throughout the country: the warehouse grocery chain stores that stock thousands of brand-name products and provide one-stop convenience. Despite the football-field-length aisles and interminable checkout lines (which can make that one stop last hours), these giant food centers are something of a necessary evil for today's busy shoppers.

But smaller food markets and other shopping sources also have a presence in Wisconsin, where places like farm markets, bakeries, and butcher shops abound. People frequent such places for many reasons: they are community based; they offer one-of-a-kind local specialties; their products can be more affordable and healthful than supermarket fare; and they provide the kind of service and people contact that's simply not available in the big stores. Look for:

- Farmers' markets and roadside stands, for seasonal produce and regional foods
- Hometown bakeries, for super-fresh baked goods, often with an ethnic twist
- Cheese factories, for unique varieties and a chance to see cheese making in progress
- Butcher shops and fish markets, for top-quality meats and gourmet items like smoked chub and whitefish livers
- Specialty producers, for goodies such as maple syrup, honey, preserves, and dried cherries
- Whole foods stores and food cooperatives, for organic choices, socially responsible foods, and bulk bargains
- Neighborhood grocery stores, for a full range of groceries with a community touch.

RASPBERRY PUFF PANCAKE

3 tablespoons butter
4 eggs
1 cup milk
1 cup flour
1 teaspoon almond
   extract
4 teaspoons raspberry
   liqueur
fresh raspberries
powdered sugar

Heat oven to 475 degrees. When oven is hot, place butter in large cast iron skillet (10 to 11 inches in diameter) and place pan in oven to melt butter. Meanwhile, combine eggs, milk, and flour in blender or food processor; blend until smooth. Add almond extract and raspberry liqueur; blend again. When butter is melted in skillet, swirl the pan to evenly coat it. Pour batter into hot skillet; bake pancake until puffed and golden, about 12 minutes. Cut pancake into four wedges immediately and serve each wedge sprinkled with fresh raspberries and powdered sugar.

Makes 4 servings.

Christine Klessig, Amherst Junction, Wisconsin

"To make individual pancakes, divide the batter evenly among four 4-inch ramekins which have been prepared with melted butter as above. Bake about 10 minutes."

TOFFEE CRUNCH APPLE MUFFINS

To make toffee streusel: Melt butter in small saucepan; remove from heat and stir in ¾ cup of the oats, ¼ cup of the brown sugar, and the baking bits. Set aside.

Heat oven to 350 degrees. Lightly grease or spray 12 muffin cups, or line them with paper liners. Combine flour, remaining 1 cup oats, baking powder, cinnamon, and salt in large bowl. In separate bowl, combine apples, sugar, remaining ¼ cup brown sugar, vegetable oil, and egg. Mix well. Add wet mixture to dry mixture; stir until just combined.

Divide batter evenly into muffin cups. Sprinkle with walnuts, then sprinkle on the toffee streusel. Bake until toothpick inserted near center of a muffin comes out clean, and tops are golden brown, 20 to 25 minutes.

Makes 12 muffins.

¼ cup (½ stick) butter or margarine

1 ¾ cups rolled oats, divided

½ cup brown sugar, divided

¼ cup English toffee baking bits

1 cup flour

1 teaspoon baking powder

½ teaspoon ground cinnamon

¼ teaspoon salt

2 cups peeled, chopped firm, tart apples

¾ cup sugar

6 tablespoons vegetable oil

1 egg

¾ cup coarsely chopped walnuts

JULIE DeMATTEO, CLEMENTON, NEW JERSEY

FRUIT AND CEREAL BREAKFAST PUDDING

....

4 cups skim or 2% milk

½ cup brown sugar

2 cups tart cherries, fresh, or frozen and thawed

3 red apples, sliced thinly

2 cups rolled oats

1 cup chopped walnuts

½ cup golden raisins

2 tablespoons sugar

¼ teaspoon cinnamon

1 pint sour cream

Heat oven to 350 degrees. Butter a large microwave-safe bowl. Place milk and brown sugar in it; heat in microwave oven 8 minutes. Stir in cherries, apples, oats, walnuts, and raisins, mixing well. Bake 30 minutes. Mix sugar and cinnamon. Serve the pudding hot or warm topped with sour cream. Sprinkle with cinnamon sugar.

Makes 8 servings.

....

JOHN KLOPFER, GAINESVILLE, FLORIDA

MASTERING THE ART

Cooking is a lifelong learning adventure, and one of the most pleasurable ways to continue one's education is to take cooking classes. Culinary schools, restaurants, cookware shops, kitchen design stores, technical colleges, minicourses, and degree programs offer everything from how to sharpen a knife to caramelizing dessert tarts with a torch. For those who have a fascination with food that goes beyond the question of what's for dinner, here's a "taste" of cooking courses around Wisconsin.

- The Cooking School at Kristofer's, Sister Bay, 920-854-9419. Demonstration and participation sessions with ethnic, regional, and other themes.
- Orange Tree Imports Cooking School, Madison, 888-245-1860 or 608-255-8211. Single-class sessions on weekday evenings covering basics to advanced learning.
- Ecole de Cuisine, Kohler, 920-451-9151. French-influenced, purist approach and intensive courses for home cooks. One-time demonstration classes and weekend or week-long packages for participation classes.
- All Through The House, Stoughton, 608-877-9403. Demonstration classes in a kitchen and gift shop setting.
- Blue Moon Cafe & Deli, Menomonie, 715-235-8596. Cooking with whole and organic foods.
- Wisconsin Union Minicourses, Madison, 608-262-3156. International, vegetarian, and "everyday" cooking instruction for people with basic skills.
- Culinary Arts Department, Fox Valley Technical College, Appleton, 920-735-5645. Credit and noncredit courses in many subjects.
- Hospitality and Tourism Department, University of Wisconsin–Stout, Menomonie, 715-232-1203. Credit courses for career track students plus continuing education for culinary professionals and serious home cooks.

TRAILS END APPLE BREAD PUDDING

4 eggs

1 1/4 cups apple juice or white grape juice

1 cup sugar

1/2 cup buttermilk

2 teaspoons vanilla extract

6 cups stale whole wheat or white bread, crusts removed, cut into cubes

3 cups peeled, chopped apples

1/2 cup dried cranberries

1/4 cup brown sugar

2 tablespoons butter or margarine, softened

1 teaspoon cinnamon

1/2 teaspoon nutmeg

sweetened whipped cream and thin apple slices (optional)

Heat oven to 350 degrees. Oil or spray a 9-inch-square baking dish. Whisk the eggs, apple juice, sugar, buttermilk, and vanilla in a bowl until well combined. Combine bread cubes, chopped apples, and dried cranberries in large bowl. Pour the wet mixture into the bread mixture and mix well. Spread into prepared baking dish. Combine brown sugar, butter, cinnamon, and nutmeg in small bowl; mix with fingertips until crumbly and sprinkle evenly over the bread pudding. Bake until knife inserted near center comes out clean, 35 to 45 minutes. Serve warm or at room temperature, with whipped cream and a garnish of apple slices, if desired.

Makes 8 servings.

Gloria Ward, Apache Junction, Arizona

BLUEBERRY CHERRY CLAFOUTI

Heat oven to 350 degrees. Butter an 11-inch round quiche pan or ovenproof dish. To make batter, combine ground oats, eggs, milk, melted butter, pumpkin pie spice, rum, and salt in food processor or blender. Process until smooth. Pour into prepared pan. Arrange fruit on top. Bake until batter is set and lightly browned, about 35 minutes. Serve warm or at room temperature, dusted with powdered sugar. To serve this as a dessert, top it with ice cream.

Makes 8 servings.

1 cup quick oats, finely ground

3 eggs

1 ¼ cups whole milk or half-and-half

4 tablespoons melted butter

1 teaspoon pumpkin pie spice

1 tablespoon rum

¼ teaspoon salt

1 ½ cups pitted sweet cherries

1 cup blueberries

1 tablespoon powdered sugar

vanilla ice cream

Loanne Chiu, Fort Worth, Texas

5

DESSERTS

"**B**ring on the dessert. I think I am about to die." Found in a book of quotations years ago, this poignant request has always reminded me of how we save the best for last. It implies that, whether for a meal or a life, what we all want is a sweet finish.

Dessert itself is a reminder that despite the many ways food functions in our lives—as sustenance, medicine, heritage, economic presence, environmental issue—there's still room in our diets for pure enjoyment. As the mouth-watering recipes in this chapter can prove, when we dig into a wedge of streusel-topped maple apple tart or down a slice of Great Aunt Annie's raspberry jelly roll, it isn't about nutrition or self-control, it's about sensual pleasure, pure and simple.

Glorious cheesecakes, rich tortes and truffles, chunky cookies, and scrumptious bars, puddings, and pies. Dessert is a celebration, a small act of self-indulgence, a means to seize the moment and feel the joy of life.

Mood-enhancing chocolate, of course, is a natural in many sweet specialties. Who wouldn't feel happy about a caramel chocolate chip cheesecake or a chocolate-glazed peanut butter pie? You'll find these and other chocolate sensations in the following pages. Still, in a state that boasts a myriad of apple festivals, hosts strawberry recipe contests, and features the lowly cranberry in a gigantic annual celebration, when it comes to desserts, the fruit's the thing.

Regional harvests include blueberries, blackberries, raspberries, rhubarb, straw-berries, cranberries, cherries, plums, pears, melons, even apricots and elderberries. Of all the seasonal fruits we cook with, however, surely apples are the most popular in desserts. Apple pies and apple tarts are only the beginning; the cooks in this chapter also came up with delicacies like apple cheddar cobbler, Bavarian apple cream tart, and caramelized apple parfaits. For out-and-out fantasy, others conjured apple torte with apple cider honey sauce and apple phyllo cups with rum raisin sauce.

Dried fruit, a growing craze on the specialty food scene, gets a local twist with dried cherries and dried cranberries. Surely raisin sales took a dive when home bakers starting adding sweet-tart dried cranberries to oatmeal cookies, and the numbers are probably still plummeting as bakers substitute plump, ruby-red dried cherries in everything from granola to polenta pie.

Honestly Good

As with appetizers, main dishes, salads, and soups, today's desserts feature "new" ingredients and trendy cooking styles. Unusual combinations found in this section, such as blue cheese and lemon juice in raspberry-accented cheesecake, or a cappuccino pudding with orange-flavored whipped cream, make for culinary artistry. But there is a flip side to the art of making desserts, for often it's the simplest things that taste the best. Try macerating juicy berries in brown sugar and balsamic vinegar, as one contributor does, and using the sauce to top premium ice cream. Or follow the lead of another, who adds common zucchini, sweetened and spiced with cinnamon, to an easy-to-make kuchen.

Dessert preparation doesn't have to be elaborate and doesn't require great finesse. But for outstanding results, what is necessary is fresh, top-quality ingredients, the kinds of "honest" foods for which Wisconsin is famous: real butter, fresh milk, maple syrup, quality chocolate, distinctive cheeses, and flavor-packed fruits.

CHOCOLATE RASPBERRY CHEESECAKE

Grand Prize Winner, 1998

Heat oven to 350 degrees. Mix cake mix and butter in large bowl until crumbly. Pat mixture over bottom and 2 inches up the sides of 10-inch springform pan.

Beat cream cheese and sugar in bowl with electric mixer for 3 minutes. Beat in eggs one at a time. Mix in sieved raspberries, vanilla, ¼ cup heavy cream, and sour cream. Pour into prepared crust. Bake until center is set, 55 to 60 minutes. Cool completely.

Bring remaining ¼ cup heavy cream just to the boil in small saucepan. Remove from heat; stir in chocolate chips until mixture is smooth. Spread over cooled cheesecake to cover filling and to meet crust edge. Cover and chill thoroughly, several hours to overnight.

Run a thin-bladed knife around cheesecake; remove pan sides. Garnish with fresh raspberries and mint.

Makes 16 servings.

1 package (18 ¼ ounces) devil's food cake mix

½ cup (1 stick) butter, softened

3 packages (each 8 ounces) cream cheese, softened

¾ cup sugar

3 eggs

1 ½ cups fresh or frozen, thawed raspberries, sieved to remove seeds

1 teaspoon vanilla extract

½ cup heavy cream, divided

¼ cup sour cream

½ cup semisweet chocolate chips

fresh raspberries and mint sprigs

LISA KEYS, MIDDLEBURY, CONNECTICUT

CARAMEL CHIP CHEESECAKE

Honorable Mention, 1997

Crust

¹/₂ cup miniature
   chocolate chips

¹/₃ cup butter

1 ¹/₂ cups uncooked
   quick oatmeal

¹/₂ cup flour

¹/₄ cup brown sugar

Filling

2 packages (each
   8 ounces) cream
   cheese, softened

²/₃ cup sugar

1 teaspoon vanilla

2 eggs

³/₄ cup miniature
   chocolate chips

¹/₃ cup caramel ice cream
   topping

1 tablespoon flour

Heat oven to 350 degrees. Oil the bottom and sides of a 9-inch springform pan. Melt chocolate chips and butter in saucepan or microwave oven. Cool slightly. Stir in oats, flour, and brown sugar; mix well. Press firmly onto bottom and one inch up the sides of pan. Bake 10 minutes. Cool completely.

Beat cream cheese, sugar, and vanilla until creamy. Add eggs, beating well. Stir in chocolate chips. Pour batter into crust. Stir caramel topping and flour in small bowl until well combined. Spoon this mixture over filling; swirl throughout filling with the blade of a knife. Bake until center is set, 45 to 50 minutes. Cool completely. Chill at least 6 hours before serving.

Makes 12 to 16 servings.

PAM RATHBUN, MADISON, WISCONSIN

LUSCIOUS LEMON BLUE CHEESE CHEESECAKE WITH RASPBERRY SAUCE

Heat oven to 325 degrees. Spray a nonstick 10-inch springform pan with cooking spray (or oil it lightly). Wrap outside of pan in aluminum foil.

To make crust: Combine crushed corn flakes or grahams and melted butter. Press mixture into bottom of prepared pan. Chill crust.

To make filling: Beat cream cheese and blue cheese in large bowl with electric mixer at medium speed until smooth. Combine flour and sugar in small bowl. Beat sugar mixture into cheese mixture at medium-low speed. Beat in eggs one at a time. Beat in sour cream, lemon extract, and lemon zest until well blended.

To bake cheesecake: Bring several cups water to boil. Pour cheese filling into prepared pan, place in another deep pan, and pour enough boiling water into bottom pan to come at least an inch up the sides of cheesecake pan. Place in center of oven and bake until center is barely set, 75 to 90 minutes. Remove cheesecake pan from bottom pan and cool cheesecake thoroughly on wire rack. Chill at least 8 hours to allow flavor to develop.

To make sauce: Pass the thawed berries through sieve to remove seeds. Combine sieved berries, jam, and lemon juice in small bowl.

Run a thin-bladed knife around sides of cheesecake and remove sides of pan. Serve each slice of cheesecake with some of the sauce spooned over it. Garnish with mint sprigs.

Makes 12 to 14 servings.

Crust
2 cups crushed corn flakes or graham crackers

$1/4$ cup melted butter

Filling
4 packages (each 8 ounces) cream cheese, softened

6 ounces blue cheese, crumbled, softened

$1/4$ cup flour

1 cup plus 2 tablespoons sugar

6 eggs

$3/4$ cup sour cream

1 $1/2$ teaspoons lemon extract

2 tablespoons grated lemon zest (grate only outermost, yellow part of the rind)

Sauce
1 package (10 ounce) frozen raspberries, thawed

5 to 6 tablespoons seedless raspberry jam

1 teaspoon lemon juice

Garnish
fresh mint sprigs

MARY LOUISE LEVER, ROME, GEORGIA

"My hobby is creating unusual desserts and this one has been a favorite for a long time."

BLUEBERRY SPIRAL DESSERT

Honorable Mention, 1998

1/4 cup (1/2 stick) butter, melted

3 cups fresh or frozen blueberries

1 teaspoon almond extract

1/2 teaspoon cinnamon

1 cup sugar

1 teaspoon honey

1 1/2 cups self-rising flour

2 teaspoons chopped walnuts

1/2 cup (1 stick) chilled butter, cut into small pieces

1/3 cup milk

sweetened whipped cream

toasted slivered almonds

Heat oven to 350 degrees. Place melted butter in 10-inch deep-dish pie plate. Gently toss blueberries, almond extract, and cinnamon in bowl. Place sugar, honey, and 1 cup water in saucepan; stir over medium heat until sugar is dissolved. Remove from heat.

Place flour, walnuts, and chilled butter in food processor; using pulse button, process until mixture resembles coarse meal. Slowly add milk; process just until dough forms.

Roll out dough on floured surface into 9-by-11-inch rectangle. Spread blueberries over dough. Roll up from narrow end; slice into 1 1/2-inch-wide "spirals." Place spirals in pie plate, tucking any berries that fall out back into dough. Drizzle melted sugar mixture over spirals. Bake until toothpick inserted in spiral comes out clean, 40 to 50 minutes. Serve warm, topped with whipped cream and sprinkled with almonds.

Makes 6 to 8 servings.

ZITA WILENSKY AND RAYMOND ROBBINS, NORTH MIAMI BEACH, FLORIDA

GREAT AUNT ANNIE'S RASPBERRY JELLY ROLL

Separate cold eggs into two large bowls (make sure the bowl for the egg whites is completely clean and dry). Allow egg whites to come to room temperature.

Heat oven to 350 degrees. Line a 9 ½-by-13 ½-inch jelly roll pan (a baking sheet with sides) with wax paper. Place sugar, cold water, vanilla, and salt in bowl with egg yolks. Beat with electric mixer until thickened. Sift the cake flour, then fold (do not beat) it into the sugar mixture. Wash and thoroughly dry the electric beaters. Beat egg whites until foamy. Sprinkle in the cream of tartar and continue beating until egg whites are stiff. Fold them into the sugar mixture. Gently spread the batter in prepared pan. Bake until cake springs back with the touch of a finger, 35 to 45 minutes.

Just before cake is done, wet a lightweight cotton towel, wring it out, and spread it on a table or counter top. When cake is done, invert it onto the damp towel and immediately peel off the wax paper. While cake is still warm, spread its entire top surface with the raspberry jam. Grasp the ends of the towel and roll up the cake horizontally (long side towards you) as tightly as possible without cracking or breaking the cake. Continue rolling until towel rolls completely off the cake. Let it cool. Sprinkle it with powdered sugar.

Place cake on long platter. Slice with a serrated knife.

Makes 12 to 15 slices of cake.

7 large farm fresh eggs (store-bought eggs can be used but will produce a paler jelly roll)
1 ½ cups sugar
3 tablespoons cold water
½ teaspoon vanilla extract
¼ teaspoon salt
1 cup cake flour
¾ teaspoon cream of tartar
1 cup raspberry jam (homemade preferred)
powdered sugar

SUSAN MARIE MATTSON, BRULE, WISCONSIN

"I've made this since I was a child; it's very good!"

CRANBERRY CAKE

Winner, Dessert Category, 1997

Cake

3 cups flour

1 ½ cups sugar

3 teaspoons baking powder

¼ teaspoon salt

1 ½ cups milk

6 tablespoons butter, melted

3 cups fresh or frozen cranberries, divided

Topping

½ cup (1 stick) butter

1 cup sugar

1 cup heavy cream

Heat oven to 350 degrees. Butter and flour a 9-by-13-inch baking pan. Combine flour, sugar, baking powder, and salt in bowl. Stir in milk, melted butter, and 2 cups of the cranberries. Spread batter into pan; sprinkle remaining cranberries over top. Bake 50 to 60 minutes, until toothpick inserted near center comes out clean. Cool.

Combine topping ingredients in saucepan; bring to boil. Spoon warm topping over cake servings. (Topping can be reheated.)

Makes 12 to 16 servings.

JANET MELBY, LA CRESCENT, MINNESOTA

NORTH WOODS MAPLE APPLE TART

To make crust: Combine flour, sugar, and baking powder in bowl. Cut in butter with pastry blender or two knives until mixture resembles coarse meal. Beat milk and egg yolk in small bowl until smooth, then stir this into flour mixture until blended. Press dough into an 8-inch-square baking pan, evenly covering the bottom and making an edge partway up the sides of the pan. Set aside.

Heat oven to 350 degrees. Peel, core, and slice the apples. Arrange the slices in the crust to make an attractive pattern. Slowly pour maple syrup evenly over apples.

To make streusel, combine flour, cinnamon, and nutmeg in small bowl. Cut in butter until mixture is crumbly. Stir in hickory nuts and sprinkle mixture evenly over the apples. Bake until apples are tender, about 35 minutes. Serve warm or at room temperature, each serving topped with a slice of cheddar, ice cream, or whipped cream.

Makes 6 servings.

Crust
- 1 1/4 cups flour
- 1 teaspoon sugar
- 1 teaspoon baking powder
- 1/2 cup (1 stick) cold butter or margarine, cut into pieces
- 2 tablespoons milk
- 1 egg yolk

Filling
- 8 to 10 apples ("Macs are nice.")
- 1/2 cup pure maple syrup

Streusel
- 1 1/2 tablespoons flour
- 1/4 teaspoon cinnamon
- 1/4 teaspoon nutmeg
- 2 tablespoons butter or margarine, cut into pieces
- 1/2 cup chopped hickory nuts

Other
- slices of cheddar cheese, ice cream, or sweetened whipped cream

Marge Breutzmann, Ocala, Florida

"The cheese can be cut into attractive patterns; cookie cutters will help."

BAVARIAN APPLE CREAM TART

Crust
1 1/4 cups flour
3/4 cup butter, softened
1/4 cup sugar
1 egg yolk

Streusel
1/2 cup flour
1/4 cup sugar
1/4 cup brown sugar
1/3 cup butter, softened
1 teaspoon cinnamon
1/4 teaspoon nutmeg

Filling
3 to 4 large baking apples (Cortland, Jonathan, or Northern Spy)
2 tablespoons fresh lemon juice
2/3 cup spiced apple wine
2 packages (each 8 ounces) cream cheese, softened
1/2 cup sugar
2 eggs
1 teaspoon vanilla extract
1/2 teaspoon almond extract
1 tablespoon flour
1/3 cup bottled caramel apple dip
3/4 cup sliced unblanched almonds

Heat oven to 400 degrees.

To make crust: Place flour, butter, sugar, and egg yolk in food processor and process just until dough forms a ball. Flour your fingers and press dough onto bottom and 1 inch up the sides of a quiche pan with removable bottom or a 10-inch springform pan. Bake 4 minutes. Remove from oven and set aside.

To make streusel topping: Mix all streusel ingredients in a small bowl until crumbly. Reserve.

To make filling: Peel and thinly slice the apples (you should have about 3 cups). Gently toss apples with lemon juice and apple wine, and let marinate 10 minutes. Place mixture in a shallow, greased baking dish and bake at 400 degrees for 10 minutes. Remove from oven, drain, and reserve.

Beat cream cheese and sugar with electric mixer on medium speed until mixture is fluffy, several minutes. Beat in eggs, vanilla, almond extract, and flour at low speed.

When mixture is thoroughly blended, spread it into the prepared crust. With a knife or thin spatula, swirl the caramel apple dip throughout the cream cheese mixture. Sprinkle sliced almonds over mixture. Spoon apple slices over almonds. Sprinkle streusel topping over apples. Bake at 400 degrees for 15 minutes, then reduce oven heat to 350 degrees and continue baking until tart is set, about 30 minutes. Cool tart completely on wire rack.

To serve, gently remove sides and transfer tart to a serving platter.

Makes 10 to 12 servings.

Josephine B. Piro, Easton, Pennsylvania

APPLE TORTE WITH APPLE CIDER HONEY SAUCE

To make torte: Heat oven to 350 degrees. Butter a 9-inch pie plate. Cream butter and sugar in bowl. Mix in egg and vanilla. Combine flour, cinnamon, baking soda, and nutmeg in separate bowl, then stir into creamed mixture. Fold in chopped apples and walnuts. Spread in prepared pie plate. Bake 40 to 45 minutes. Cool torte to warm temperature.

To make cider honey sauce: Combine apple cider, honey, lemon zest, lemon juice, cornstarch, and nutmeg in saucepan. Mix well. Cook over medium heat, stirring constantly, until bubbly and thickened. Stir in butter until melted.

Serve each piece of warm torte with some of the sauce ladled over the top.

Makes 6 to 8 servings.

Torte
1/4 cup (1/2 stick) butter, softened
1 cup sugar
1 egg
2 teaspoons vanilla extract
1 cup flour
2 teaspoons cinnamon
1 teaspoon baking soda
1/4 teaspoon ground nutmeg
2 cups peeled, finely chopped tart apples
1/2 cup finely chopped walnuts

Cider Honey Sauce
1 cup apple cider
1/3 cup honey
1/2 teaspoon grated lemon zest (grate only outermost, yellow part of the rind)
2 tablespoons lemon juice
1 tablespoon cornstarch
1/4 teaspoon nutmeg
3 tablespoons butter, cut into pieces

Rosemary Garber, Windsor, Wisconsin

EAT THEIR WORDS

For something so profoundly central to our lives, food has been woefully neglected as a subject of academic study. In the American education system, nutrition gets minimal attention while "cuisine appreciation" courses—unlike art or music—are practically nonexistent. Things are different in popular culture, however. Consider the explosive demand for cookbooks, culinary magazines, food newsletters, and epicurean Web sites. Indeed, these days it almost seems as if the less time we have to prepare food, the more we want to read about it.

What's more, it isn't just recipes and restaurant reviews we're poring over; it's food history, food travel, food folklore, food memoir, food science, food literature. People who enjoy a tale about the cherry harvest in Door County or the origins of Danish kringle know that food is much more than recipes; it's a fascinating doorway to important knowledge about ourselves and our world.

Happily, increasing numbers of authors give food the literary attention it deserves. For some deliciously enlightening reading, consider these publications by some of America's finest food writers:

- *A Well-Seasoned Appetite*, by Molly O'Neill
- *Blue Corn and Chocolate*, by Elisabeth Rozin
- *Fading Feast* and *Why We Eat What We Eat*, by Raymond Sokolov
- *On Food and Cooking*, by Harold McGee
- *Home Cooking* and *More Home Cooking*, by Laurie Colwin
- *I Hear America Cooking*, by Betty Fussell
- *Tender at the Bone*, by Ruth Reichl
- *The Tummy Trilogy*, by Calvin Trillin
- *The Art of Eating* (newsletter), by Edward Behr
- *Anything*, by M. F. K. Fisher.

CHERRY LEMONADE TART

Heat oven to 350 degrees.

To make crust: Combine flour and ginger in large bowl. Cut in butter with pastry blender or two knives until mixture resembles coarse meal. Spread mixture on bottom and up the sides of a 9-inch pie pan. Press firmly to form a firm crust. Bake until lightly browned, about 20 minutes. Cool on wire rack.

To make filling: Whisk egg, sugar, lemon zest, lemon juice, flour, and baking powder in a bowl. Stir in drained cherries. Pour mixture into cooled crust. Sprinkle coconut on top. Bake until filling is set, about 35 minutes. Cool on wire rack. Sift powdered sugar over cooled tart.

Makes 8 servings.

Crust
1 1/3 cups flour
1/2 teaspoon ground ginger
1/2 cup (1 stick) butter, softened

Filling
1 egg, beaten
1/2 cup sugar
1/2 teaspoon grated lemon zest (grate only outermost, yellow part of the peel)
1/4 cup fresh lemon juice
1 tablespoon flour
1/4 teaspoon baking powder
1 can (16 ounces) pitted tart cherries (not cherry pie filling), drained
1/3 cup sweetened flaked coconut
1 to 2 tablespoons powdered sugar

Rema Conger, Tulsa, Oklahoma

ZUCCHINI KUCHEN

Honorable Mention, 1997

8 cups peeled, seeded, and chopped zucchini (about 4 pounds whole zucchini)

²/₃ cup fresh lemon juice

3 cups sugar, divided

2 teaspoons cinnamon, divided

½ teaspoon nutmeg

4 cups flour

1 ½ cups (3 sticks) cold butter, in small pieces

Combine zucchini and lemon juice in saucepan; cook over medium heat, stirring often, until tender, 15 to 20 minutes. Stir in 1 cup of the sugar, 1 teaspoon of the cinnamon, and the nutmeg; simmer 1 minute longer. Remove from heat. Heat oven to 375 degrees. Butter a 9-by-13-inch baking pan.

To make crust: Combine flour and remaining 2 cups of sugar in bowl. Cut in butter until mixture resembles coarse crumbs. Stir ½ cup of this mixture into zucchini. Press half the remaining flour mixture into baking pan. Spread zucchini mixture over crust. Crumble remaining flour mixture over zucchini. Sprinkle with remaining cinnamon. Bake until lightly browned and bubbly, 35 to 45 minutes. Serve warm, with ice cream if desired.

Makes 12 servings.

PAT MORRIS, LYNDON STATION, WISCONSIN

CRUNCHY APPLE CHEDDAR COBBLER

Honorable Mention, 1998

Heat oven to 400 degrees. Oil a 9-inch-square baking pan.

To make apple layer: Combine sugar, flour, and cinnamon in bowl. Toss in apples, dried cherries, and cashews. Place in baking pan. Mix cheddar, flour, brown sugar, baking powder, and salt in large bowl. Mix melted butter and milk in small bowl; stir into flour mixture. Spoon over apple mixture. Bake until puffed and golden, 25 to 30 minutes. Serve warm with whipped cream or ice cream.

Makes 8 servings.

Apple Layer

1 cup sugar

1/4 cup flour

1/4 teaspoon cinnamon

6 cups peeled and thinly sliced firm, tart apples

1/2 cup dried cherries

1/2 cup cashew halves

Topping

1 1/2 cups shredded cheddar cheese

1 cup flour

1/2 cup packed brown sugar

1 1/2 teaspoons baking powder

1/2 teaspoon salt

1/3 cup butter, melted

1/4 cup milk

Other

whipped cream or ice cream

LINDA KAY DRYSDALE, RIVERDALE, MICHIGAN

CHERRY POLENTA PIE

Honorable Mention, 1998

1 tablespoon unsalted butter, softened

6 ounces (1 ¼ cups) dried cherries

1 teaspoon salt

1 cup yellow cornmeal

⅓ cup slivered almonds

1 tablespoon cinnamon sugar

sweetened whipped cream

fresh Wisconsin cherries

Spread softened butter into a pie plate. Place dried cherries in bowl; add warm water to cover; let stand until cherries "plump," about 10 minutes. Drain cherries, measuring the liquid into large, heavy-bottomed saucepan. Add additional water to make 4 cups total. Bring to boil over high heat; stir in salt.

Heat broiler. Using a wooden spoon, stir boiling liquid with one hand while you add cornmeal in a fine stream with other hand. Keep stirring after all the cornmeal has been added until mixture is thick, smooth, and somewhat elastic, 5 to 10 minutes. Stir in plumped cherries. Spread polenta in pie plate. Sprinkle with almonds and cinnamon sugar. Heat in broiler until sugar darkens, 1 to 2 minutes.

Cut into wedges and serve warm topped with whipped cream and fresh cherries (this can also be served as a side dish if you eliminate the last three ingredients).

Makes 6 servings.

Ellen Burr, Truro, Massachusetts

CHOCOLATE-GLAZED PEANUT BUTTER PIE

To make crust: Mix crushed vanilla wafers, pecans, melted butter, sugar, and cinnamon in bowl. Press mixture onto bottom and sides of a 9-inch pie plate. Freeze crust while you make the filling.

To make filling: Beat whipping cream with electric beaters at medium speed until cream thickens and begins to form soft peaks. Gradually add ⅓ cup of the powdered sugar, then the vanilla, as you continue beating. Beat just until firm peaks form. In a separate large bowl, beat peanut butter, cream cheese, and remaining ½ cup powdered sugar until smooth. Stir about one-fourth of the whipped cream into the peanut butter mixture, then gently fold in the remaining cream until barely combined. Spread filling in prepared pie crust. Refrigerate until firm, 2 or more hours.

To make glaze: Bring whipping cream to boil in small saucepan. Remove from heat and stir in chopped chocolate until mixture is smooth. Let cool 2 to 3 minutes. Pour glaze over the pie, tilting pan to coat the surface completely. Chill the pie to set the glaze. Serve chilled.

Makes 10 to 12 servings.

GRETCHEN KELLY, HOLMEN, WISCONSIN

Crust
1 cup crushed vanilla wafer cookies
½ cup finely chopped pecans
6 tablespoons melted butter
2 tablespoons sugar
¼ teaspoon cinnamon

Filling
1 cup whipping or heavy cream
⅚ cup powdered sugar, divided
1 teaspoon vanilla extract
1 ¼ cups peanut butter
1 package (8 ounces) cream cheese, softened

Glaze
½ cup whipping or heavy cream
4 ounces finely chopped semisweet chocolate (about ⅔ cup)

APPLE PHYLLO CUPS WITH RUM RAISIN SAUCE

···

Apple Phyllo Cups

4 sheets thawed phyllo dough (thaw according to directions on package)

$1/4$ cup sugar

1 teaspoon cinnamon

6 small tart cooking apples, or 4 to 5 large ones, peeled

$1/4$ cup melted butter

$1/3$ cup slivered almonds

Rum Raisin Sauce

$1/4$ cup packed brown sugar

2 teaspoons cornstarch

$1/3$ cup golden raisins

1 tablespoon rum

Other

vanilla ice cream

2 tablespoons slivered almonds

Remove phyllo dough package (but do not open it) from refrigerator 1 hour before proceeding with recipe to allow dough to come to room temperature. Meanwhile, combine sugar and cinnamon in small bowl. Peel the apples, and if you are using 6 small ones, core them. (If you're using larger apples, core and cut them into uniform slices.) Immerse apples in water to prevent them from darkening. Butter six 6-ounce custard cups. Heat oven to 375 degrees.

Open phyllo dough package and unfold the layered dough. Lay one sheet phyllo dough on a dry surface and brush lightly with melted butter. Repeat with three more sheets of dough and remaining butter, stacking the sheets. (The remaining dough can be refolded and refrigerated; use within 1 week.) Cut the stack into six strips lengthwise and into three sections crosswise. You should have 18 rectangles. Press three rectangles into each of the prepared custard cups, angling them so that the entire surface of inner cup is covered.

Cut the small apples into thin slices about three-fourths of the way through the apple (do not cut all the way through). Place an apple in each of the dough-lined cups. (If you are using larger, sliced apples, arrange the slices in a spiral pattern in each cup.) Sprinkle apples with the cinnamon-sugar mixture; portion the slivered almonds into the cavities. Place apple phyllo cups on a large baking sheet and bake until phyllo is golden brown and apples are tender, 25 to 35 minutes.

Meanwhile, to prepare rum raisin sauce, combine brown sugar, cornstarch, raisins, and rum with $1/3$ cup water in a small saucepan. Bring to simmer, stirring constantly, and cook until thickened.

When apple phyllo cups are done, let them cool slightly, then carefully slip them onto dessert plates. They may be served warm or at room temperature. Place a scoop of ice cream on each apple cup and drizzle with warm rum raisin sauce. Garnish with additional slivered almonds.

Makes 6 servings.

MARIE RIZZIO, TRAVERSE CITY, MICHIGAN

CARAMELIZED APPLE PARFAITS

2 large tart apples

cooking spray or 2 teaspoons butter

⅓ cup sugar

2 cups vanilla yogurt, divided

1 teaspoon cinnamon

1 cup crushed gingersnap cookies

1 sweet, crisp red apple

sweetened whipped cream

Peel and dice tart apples. Spray a skillet with cooking spray (or add butter to skillet) and heat over medium-high flame. Add apples and sprinkle evenly with the sugar; do not stir. Cook until sugar melts and begins to color, about 5 minutes. Stir gently and continue cooking until apples are tender, 3 to 5 minutes. Stir in 2 tablespoons of the yogurt. Let apples cool.

Blend the remaining yogurt with the cinnamon. Into each of four wine glasses, layer one-eighth of the apples, ¼ cup yogurt mixture, and 2 tablespoons crushed gingersnaps. Repeat layers. Chill the parfaits thoroughly.

Just before serving, core (do not peel) and thinly slice the red apple. Garnish each parfait with whipped cream and red apple slices.

Makes 4 servings.

LISA KEYS, MIDDLEBURY, CONNECTICUT

CIVILIZED CHEESE

At a cooking school I attended years ago, the wine instructor was a well-traveled, educated French connoisseur who had some surprisingly parochial ideas about the Midwest. Told I was a native of Wisconsin, for example, he asked me what it was like growing up on a ranch. Something he did know about the state, however, was its reputation for dairy products. Proud of his knowledge of cheese, he mentioned that one of the most "exotic" types he'd tasted was colby—which I practically had been weaned on. My familiarity with it left this worldly man as awestruck and envious as a child meeting the owner of a candy factory.

In the Dairy State, of course, colby is not exactly exotic (although old-fashioned longhorn colby is getting rare). While much of the two billion pounds of cheese produced here annually are common varieties such as colby, mozzarella, and cheddar, we also boast numerous specialty cheeses. Here are some outstanding artisanal choices (should you ever need to impress a sophisticate from your past):

- Mascarpone: triple cream fresh cheese; sweet, buttery flavor and satiny texture
- Gorgonzola: aged blue cheese with blue-green veins; earthy sweetness and crumbly texture
- Sweet-style Swiss: smooth, rich cross between baby Swiss and stronger flavored Emmenthaler; pale golden color, nutty taste
- Queso Blanco: pure white, crumbly, nonmelting, with some salinity; used in many Latino dishes
- Limburger: semisoft, surface ripened; skunky odor; goes from mild to powerfully pungent-tasting with age
- Feta: brined, white, pleasantly salty, soft and crumbly; those made with goat or sheep milk are distinctly tangy.

CAPPUCCINO PUDDING WITH ORANGE WHIPPED CREAM

••

Pudding

3 cups whole milk

$\frac{1}{2}$ cup sugar

$\frac{1}{3}$ cup cornstarch

3 tablespoons instant coffee granules

dash of cinnamon

2 teaspoons vanilla extract

1 ounce semisweet chocolate, chopped

1 whole egg plus 1 egg white

Cream Topping

1 cup whipping cream

$\frac{1}{2}$ cup powdered sugar

1 teaspoon grated orange zest (grate only outermost, orange part of the peel)

Garnish

1 bar (1.4 ounces) milk chocolate English toffee

1 teaspoon instant coffee granules

To make pudding: Whisk milk, sugar, cornstarch, 3 tablespoons coffee granules, and cinnamon in medium saucepan. Cook over medium heat, stirring frequently, until thickened. Remove from heat and stir in vanilla and chocolate until smooth. Beat egg and egg white in a small bowl with a whisk; gradually add ½ cup of the hot pudding mixture into the eggs, whisking constantly. Whisk the egg-pudding mixture back into the saucepan. Place over medium heat and cook, stirring constantly, until thick and bubbly, 2 to 3 minutes. Let cool to warm temperature, whisking frequently to prevent "skin" from forming on surface. Divide pudding into 6 serving dishes or stemmed glasses; cover each with a piece of plastic and chill thoroughly.

To make cream topping: Chill a medium bowl and beaters. Combine whipping cream, powdered sugar, and orange zest in the chilled bowl; beat until stiff peaks form.

For garnish: Place the toffee bar in a bag and crush the toffee with the flat of a heavy utensil until candy is crumbly. Toss it with 1 teaspoon coffee granules.

To serve, top each pudding with a large dollop of whipped cream and sprinkle with crumbled toffee mixture.

Makes 6 servings.

••

SHELLY PLATTEN, AMHERST, WISCONSIN

CANDY BAR APPLE DESSERT SALAD

Chop apples into small pieces. Dice candy bars. Combine apples, candy bars, and marshmallows in large bowl. Fold in whipped cream. Garnish with sliced banana. This creation is for kids of all ages.

Makes 12 to 16 servings.

5 green apples

5 red apples

5 miniature (2.07 ounces) Snickers candy bars

1 cup miniature marshmallows

4 to 5 cups lightly sweetened whipped cream, or 1 container (12 ounces) whipped topping

1 banana

TARA L. MEFFERT, WAUNAKEE, WISCONSIN

"The taste of down-home Wisconsin-grown apples makes this salad surely 'moo-velous!'"

BOUNTIFUL BERRY DESSERT SAUCE

Winner, 1998

1 orange
1 lemon
1 lime
1 cup packed brown
    sugar
1 cup balsamic vinegar
½ cup dried cranberries
1 pint each fresh
    strawberries,
    raspberries,
    blueberries,
    blackberries
sugar (optional)

Finely grate the zest (grate only the colored part of rind) from the orange, lemon, and lime. Place zest in saucepan. Squeeze juice from all three fruits into pan. Stir in brown sugar and vinegar. Heat slowly, stirring, until sugar dissolves. Add cranberries. Cool. Cover and refrigerate at least 1 hour.

Combine all berries in large bowl. Add sugar to taste, or none at all, depending on sweetness of berries. About 1 hour before serving, gently toss berries with chilled sauce. Chill until ready to serve. Spoon over ice cream, frozen yogurt, pound cake, or angel food cake.

Makes 10 to 12 servings.

MARY CUMMINGS, NEW SMYRNA BEACH, FLORIDA

DELIGHTFUL DOUBLE BERRY FREEZE

Combine strawberries, blueberries, half-and-half, corn syrup, and lemon juice in large bowl. In separate clean, dry bowl, beat egg whites with electric beaters until fluffy, 1 to 2 minutes. Continue beating while gradually adding the powdered sugar; beat until egg whites are stiff and glossy, 2 to 3 minutes. Fold whipped egg whites into berry mixture. Gently spread mixture in 8-inch-square dish. Freeze until firm, 3 to 4 hours.

Transfer frozen mixture to large bowl. Beat with electric beaters at lowest speed for 3 minutes. Raise to high speed and beat until creamy smooth. Return mixture to pan and freeze again until firm. Serve the berry freeze in crystal bowls garnished with fresh mint sprigs.

Makes 6 to 8 servings.

1 cup mashed ripe strawberries
1 cup mashed ripe blueberries
1 cup half-and-half
$3/4$ cup light corn syrup
1 tablespoon fresh lemon juice
2 large egg whites*
$1/2$ cup powdered sugar
fresh mint sprigs
*Preferably from a local, organic source, to avoid the small risk of salmonella.

Tom Davis, Waynesboro, Mississippi

CHERRY TRUFFLES

1 package (8 ounces)
cream cheese,
softened
4 cups powdered sugar
6 ounces semisweet
chocolate morsels
(about 1 cup), melted
½ teaspoon almond
extract
24 to 36 large fresh tart
cherries, pitted
1 cup finely chopped
toasted almonds

Beat cream cheese and powdered sugar in large bowl until smooth. Add melted chocolate and almond extract; mix well. Chill until mixture is firm enough to work with, at least 1 hour. Pat cherries with paper towels to dry them well. Shape a little of the chocolate-cheese mixture around each cherry. Roll cherries in chopped nuts. Place in small paper cups and chill until ready to serve.

Makes 24 to 36 truffles.

ROXANNE E. CHAN, ALBANY, CALIFORNIA

CENTURY 21

What's ahead for food and cooking in the coming years? While fast food is here to stay, the demand for *high-quality* fast food is likely to mushroom. People want fresher, tastier food even if they don't have the time to make it themselves. Home Replacement Meals (called HMRs in the food industry) have moved beyond burger chains to include gourmet take-out and ready-to-eat "home-style" meals from the supermarket. Trends like personal home chefs and Internet shopping for upscale groceries are also surfacing.

Whether we cook at home or grab it and go, we want "fast" food that tastes "slow." We also want it to be good for us and for the environment. We'll keep an eye on fat and cholesterol while we look more to "nutraceutical" foods like broccoli to help boost our immune systems. Organic and heirloom produce is gaining popularity, and we're increasingly interested in issues like biodiversity and sustainability.

As always, trendy ingredients will come and go. Some favored foods, like soy-based and kosher products, will address health concerns, while others, perhaps flavored salts and specialty sugars, will help satisfy our passion for the exotic. Ethnic cuisine should flourish, given that the United States is more demographically diverse than ever before. We'll look to television's celebrity chefs and the Internet for culinary entertainment, and the more we understand the myriad ways that food affects—and defines—us, the more we'll incorporate food studies into our educational system.

By now we've tried just about everything. As for the future, surely anything goes.

CHERRY CHIP COOKIES

Winner, 1998

1 cup (2 sticks) butter, softened

²/₃ cup brown sugar

1 ¹/₃ cups sugar

2 eggs

1 ¹/₂ teaspoons vanilla extract

3 cups flour

1 teaspoon baking soda

1 teaspoon salt

2 cups dried cherries

2 cups chopped walnuts

1 ¹/₂ cups chocolate chips

1 ¹/₂ cups white chocolate chips

Heat oven to 325 degrees. Oil baking sheets or line them with parchment paper. Cream butter and sugars in large bowl. Beat in eggs and vanilla. In another bowl, combine flour, baking soda, and salt. Stir this into butter mixture and mix well. Stir in cherries, walnuts, chocolate chips, and white chocolate chips. Drop dough in 3-tablespoon portions onto prepared baking sheets, leaving 1 to 2 inches between cookies. Bake 14 to 16 minutes. Cool cookies on baking sheets 5 minutes, then cool completely on racks.

Makes 50 to 60 cookies.

KRISTINE DITTMANN, DOUSMAN, WISCONSIN

GRANOLA DRIED CRANBERRY COOKIES

Heat oven to 350 degrees. Lightly grease two baking sheets or line them with parchment paper. Cream butter and brown sugar in large bowl. Add honey, eggs, and vanilla; beat until light and fluffy. In another bowl, combine flour, baking soda, baking powder, and cinnamon. Stir this into the butter mixture and beat until well blended. Stir in granola, oats, and dried cranberries. Drop batter by spoonfuls onto prepared baking sheets. Bake cookies until lightly browned, 10 to 12 minutes. Cool on wire racks.

Makes 5 dozen cookies.

½ cup (1 stick) butter, softened
1 cup dark brown sugar
⅓ cup honey
2 eggs or equivalent egg substitute
1 teaspoon vanilla
2 cups flour
½ teaspoon baking soda
½ teaspoon baking powder
1 teaspoon cinnamon
2 cups low-fat granola cereal
1 cup uncooked oats
1 cup dried cranberries

NANCY F. RAFAL, BAILEYS HARBOR, WISCONSIN

"I've been 'improving' this recipe for several years and this is the best version to date."

CARAMEL CRANBERRY OAT BARS

1 cup fresh or frozen
    cranberries
½ cup sugar
2 ½ cups flour, divided
2 cups oats
½ cup packed light
    brown sugar
½ teaspoon baking soda
1 cup (2 sticks) melted
    butter
1 ½ cups chopped dates
¾ cup chopped walnuts
1 cup bottled caramel
    topping

Heat oven to 350 degrees. Mix cranberries, sugar, 2 cups of the flour, oats, brown sugar, and baking soda in large bowl. Stir in butter; mix until crumbly. Reserve 1 cup of the mixture; press the remainder firmly and evenly onto bottom of 13-by-9-inch pan. Bake 15 minutes.

Remove pan from oven and sprinkle dates and walnuts over crust. Mix caramel topping and remaining ½ cup flour and drizzle this mixture over dates and nuts. Sprinkle reserved cranberry mixture over caramel. Bake until light brown, about 20 minutes. Cool and cut into bars.

Makes 24 bars.

Kathryn Grefe, Mauston, Wisconsin

MAPLE DRIED CRANBERRY DROP COOKIES

Heat oven to 350 degrees. Beat butter and maple syrup in large bowl until well combined. Beat in eggs and vanilla. In a separate bowl, mix flour, wheat germ (if desired), baking soda, cinnamon, cardamom, and salt. Stir flour mixture into butter mixture until well combined. Stir in oats and dried cranberries. Drop by heaping tablespoonfuls onto ungreased baking sheets. Bake 10 to 11 minutes. Cool on wire racks.

Makes 3 ½ to 4 dozen cookies.

½ cup (1 stick) butter or margarine, at room temperature

1 cup pure maple syrup

2 eggs

1 teaspoon vanilla extract

2 cups flour

1 tablespoon toasted wheat germ (optional)

1 teaspoon baking soda

1 teaspoon cinnamon

½ teaspoon ground cardamom

½ teaspoon salt

3 cups uncooked oats

1 cup dried cranberries

STEPHANIE FINCH, BARABOO, WISCONSIN

FUDGE NUT ICE CREAM PIE

2 egg whites
½ teaspoon cream of tartar
½ cup sugar
1 ½ cups chopped walnuts
1 ½ pints fudge nut ice cream
2 squares (each 1 ounce) semi-sweet chocolate
1 cup sweetened condensed milk
sweetened whipped cream (optional)

Heat oven to 300 degrees. Butter a 10-inch deep-dish pie pan. Place egg whites and cream of tartar in clean bowl. Beat at medium speed with electric beaters while slowly adding the sugar. Beat until egg whites are stiff. Fold in chopped walnuts. Spread mixture in prepared pie pan. Bake 50 minutes; set aside to cool completely.

Soften the ice cream about 30 minutes in the refrigerator. Spoon softened ice cream into cooled pie shell. Spread to even out the surface. Cover with wax paper and freeze until firm.

To make topping: Melt the chocolate in a double boiler. Stir in sweetened condensed milk until thickened. Cool.

When topping is cool, spread it over surface of the frozen ice cream pie. Return pie to freezer until ready to serve. Remove pie from freezer 10 minutes before serving. Cut into slices and serve with whipped cream, if desired.

Makes 8 to 10 servings.

IDA FRIZZELL, AMHERST, WISCONSIN

INDEX

MORE GREAT TITLES FROM TRAILS BOOKS

Activities

Paddling Illinois: 64 Great Trips by Canoe and Kayak, Mike Svob

Paddling Northern Wisconsin: 82 Great Trips by Canoe and Kayak, Mike Svob

Great Minnesota Walks: 49 Strolls, Rambles, Hikes, and Treks, Wm. Chad McGrath

Great Wisconsin Walks: 45 Strolls, Rambles, Hikes, and Treks, Wm. Chad McGrath

Best Canoe Trails of Southern Wisconsin, Michael E. Duncanson

Best Wisconsin Bike Trips, Phil Van Valkenberg

Travel Guides

The Spirit of Door County: A Photographic Essay, Darryl R. Beers

Up North Wisconsin: A Region for All Seasons, Sharyn Alden

Great Wisconsin Taverns: 101 Distinctive Badger Bars, Dennis Boyer

Great Wisconsin Restaurants, Dennis Getto

Great Weekend Adventures, the Editors of Wisconsin Trails

County Parks of Wisconsin: 600 Parks You Can Visit, Jeannette Bell and Chet Bell

The Wisconsin Traveler's Companion: A Guide to Country Sights, Jerry Apps and Julie
   Sutter-Blair

Home and Garden

Creating a Perennial Garden in the Midwest, Joan Severa

Foods That Made Wisconsin Famous, Richard J. Baumann

History

Walking Tours of Wisconsin's Historic Towns, Lucy Rhodes, Elizabeth McBride, and Anita Matcha

Wisconsin: The Story of the Badger State, Norman K. Risjord

Barns of Wisconsin, Jerry Apps

Portrait of the Past: A Photographic Journey Through Wisconsin, 1865–1920, Howard Mead,
   Jill Dean, and Susan Smith

For Young People

Wisconsin Portraits: 55 People Who Made a Difference, Martin Hintz

ABCs of Wisconsin, Dori Hillestad Butler and Alison Relyea

W Is for Wisconsin, Dori Hillestad Butler and Eileen Dawson

Other Titles of Interest

The I-Files: True Reports of Unexplained Phenomena in Illinois, Jay Rath

The W-Files: True Reports of Wisconsin's Unexplained Phenomena, Jay Rath

The M-Files: True Reports of Minnesota's Unexplained Phenomena, Jay Rath

For a free catalog, phone, write, or e-mail us.

Trails Books
P.O. Box 317, Black Earth, WI 53515
(800) 236-8088
e-mail: info@wistrails.com
www.trailsbooks.com